12 UNDENIABLE LAWS FOR SEX

WHAT THE BIBLE SAYS THAT CAN MAKE YOUR SEX MANIFEST HEAVEN ON EARTH

BY: TIFFANY DOMENA

WHAT OTHERS ARE SAYING

"We live in a society where we tend to take sex lightly and it has caused so many problems and heartache. The 12 Undeniable Laws of Sex will reveal to you how important it is to do things God's way and what happens when we step outside of God's will. This book is truly a blessing to all; if you are married, single or for your teenagers you need a copy. It will help dispel the untruths about sex and bring deliverance to those who are in unhealthy sexual addictions or in bondage from past sexual sins. I highly recommend this book and it has truly been a blessing to me."

- Deborah Dunson, Woman of God and Prayer Warrior

"Well that is probably the deepest book on Sex I have ever read. Raw, Real, and Revealing".

- Letty Donald, Woman of God and Internet Marketing Guru

"A Must Read For Everyone!! I was given the opportunity to read this book through the generosity of the author Tiffany Domena. I was not sure what to expect based upon the title. It is one of the most important books I've read on human sexuality from a spiritual perspective. There are brief paragraphs at the beginning of each chapter that describe different scenarios one might find themselves in as born-again believers. Tiffany writes from a place of deep truth that is rarely found in books of this kind. I found it to be bold and refreshing. I would recommend this as a study for Sunday School, bible study or small groups. There is vitally important information shared and you would do yourself a huge disservice by not reading this book. I learned a number of things about sexuality God's way. It's time to reclaim this area of our life so that we might be instruments of change in the kingdom."

-Tawana Hawkins, Women's Spiritual Growth Mentor

TABLE OF CONTENTS

PREFACE

Whether you like it or not, whether you have had sex or not, sex has changed you. You walk around everyday either guarded or loose because of how you were groomed about sex. You treat people with kindness or distrust because of how you have seen sex valued in relationships. To better explain what I mean, let me tell you the story of Amanda and Taniesha.

Amanda and Taniesha were classmates in the fourth grade. They lived within ten minutes of one another. Amanda grew up with a very intelligent and highly educated single mom while Taniesha grew up with a loving couple.

Amanda's mother prostituted prestigious men for money, and many times she would see or hear her mother with men. She saw her mother beat, yelled at, thrown out, and incapacitated because of drugs. On several occasions, when her mom was completely oblivious because of her drug intake, Amanda was raped. In the classroom, Amanda was very guarded with men and very seeking of female companionship. She was unfamiliar with proximity discomforts, and her classmates complained many times saying, "Amanda got too close in my face!". She had a very difficult time trusting that people would do good things, so her relationships were always damaged.

Taniesha sat in the same fourth grade classroom as Amanda. At home, Taniesha saw her parents always displaying affection towards one another. Sex was sacred and was not permitted to be watched or discussed loosely. Nakedness was guarded and touching between the shoulders and the thighs was considered off limits for anyone with the exception of your spouse. In relationships, Taniesha was taught to emulate love and forgiveness, and learned how to do so from the example that she saw of her mom and dad who overcame disagreements peacefully every day. In the classroom, Taniesha was developing many relationships, she was very well liked, and her classmates always talked about her virtuous character.

Similar to the story of Amanda and Taniesha, your views towards sex affect you daily. How your family taught you to value sex affects every relationship that you enter. You are either guarded or loose as a result of how sex has been treated in your life.

The subject of sex has generated so much controversy! In a secular conversation, sex is magnetizing, hypnotizing, and the subject of much attention. Meanwhile in educational and religious circles, sex is shameful, something minimally explained, and highly guarded. Despite how many veils and tarps that we attempt to use to cover the body, how many statistics we share as scare tactics, the talk of modesty that we try to stuff down everyone's throats in attempts to hide the lead magnet, or the boring materials that have been passed out to minimally educate; it is not enough! Everyone is at the point now that they want to know and understand the real "*why*".

- Why is sex so good?
- How can it get better?
- Why does the Bible present such rules about sex?
- Why is sex still good when the rules are broken?
- Why don't I see the consequences?

- How impacting are the consequences of sex?
- And many, many more questions

"Avoid sex!", was the answer of the past. Reality says "Sex is something that affects each and every one of our lives! How can we ignore that?" The Guttmacher Institute, an organization that provides sexual education reported that in the US half of teens between the ages of 15 and 19 have had sex at least once! Many of the adolescents have never heard what the Bible has to say about sex, so where do you think the adolescents are getting their ideas from? They are watching someone! Even worse, the numbers are skewed by conflicting definitions of virginity. In their article, Facts on American Teens' Sexual and Reproductive Health, The Guttmacher Institute, reported:

- More than eight out of 10 teens (83.5 percent) believed they were still virgins if they had participated in genital touching.

- More than two out of three teens (70.6 percent) believed they would still be virgins if they had had oral sex.

- About one in six teens (16.1 percent) believed they could have anal sex and still be virgins.

- About one in 20 teens (5.8 percent) thought they could have vaginal intercourse and remain virgins.[1]

From a biblical perspective, sex is being mistreated at astronomical numbers. The unfortunate truth is that people do not know what biblical sex looks like. If you think that the statistics of teenagers participating in or experiencing an interest in sex is high, how much higher do you think the statistic of adult interest in sex would be? How many of them do you think apply a biblical perspective of sex in their lives? With the divorce rates being so

1 http://www.teenhealthfx.com/answers/sexuality+sexual+health/46785

high and the marriage satisfaction rates being so low, I can frankly assure that most people do not know how to use sex to manifest Heaven on Earth. It's my observation that many adults are being visited by sexual dreams, they experience highly hyper or hypo sensitive sexual recollections, or they carry very guarded attitudes towards their fellow men and women; all because of their sexual experiences. Good or bad, sex is transformational, and this book is intended to make the transformation a good one. In this book, I intend to clear many mysteries, explain the biblical perspectives on sex, and show how you can use them to manifest Heaven on Earth thru your sexual practices. This book reaches beyond the physical arena, and provides explanation on spiritual matters that are influenced by sex. The intent in writing this book is to arm you with wisdom, so that you can understand the spiritual mysteries that most people are naively submitting to, granting access to torment, and living unfulfilled in their relationships and in their sex lives. This book will give you:

- 12 Undeniable laws for sex that manifests Heaven on Earth

- Stories to subconsciously reprogram your mind

- Facts about sex for you to extrapolate and gain further wisdom

- A divine commission for restored holiness in your sexual experience

- And, much more inside...

INTRODUCTION

Most readers are probably wondering what qualifies me to speak on this topic. The truth is that I'm not much different than you. I've had experience as well as Bible application and lots of wisdom seeking. I've had a lot of pleasure and pain with regards to the topic of sex. And, many people have shared their experiences with me. In this book, I share many lessons with you from my own first-hand experiences, as well as those of others who have spoken to me, in the hope that you will be able to avoid some of the pain that I have had. The stories that I tell don't include the names of real people, but they are real stories. Since real people experienced a range of things, you can learn from their ups and their downs. Take to heart that sex is the ceremony of a covenant being made, and the covenant can be with a spirit of good or bad. I have seen and experienced both.

A friend of mine, Life Coach Tiffany Kelly and I were taking a 20-hour ministry road trip. Throughout our trip, we shared many stories of the positive and negative impact that sex had on our own lives, those of our families and many others whose lives we have been able to observe. As we talked about the topic of sex - the things that act as lead magnets, the illusions that we have been misled by, and the rampant attack of others in very sly and subliminal ways - the passion just bubbled up within me. I have seen many people experience overwhelming joy, severe guilt and shame as a result of their perspectives on sex. I felt compelled to write this book in an effort to provide others with an opportunity to experience the joy of sex as God desires for us to have.

May this book be a blessing to you. May it align your views of sex with the will of God, and may you experience God's original plan for sex in Jesus' name!

-Tiffany Domena

CHAPTER ONE

EVERYTHING THAT FEELS GOOD IS NOT RIGHT

"Woe to those who call evil good and good evil, who put darkness for light and light for darkness, who put bitter for sweet and sweet for bitter. Woe to those who are wise in their own eyes and clever in their own sight. Woe to those who are heroes at drinking wine and champions at mixing drinks, who acquit the guilty for a bribe, but deny justice to the innocent. Therefore, as tongues of fire lick up straw and as dry grass sinks down in the flames, so their roots will decay and their flowers blow away like dust;for they have rejected the law of the LORD Almighty and spurned the word of the Holy One of Israel."

-Isaiah 5:20-24

Hester and Kirsten have been in a relationship for 15 years and married for five years. As soon as the homosexual laws passed in their area, they immediately went to make their relationship official as a marriage. Both of them had previous heterosexual relationships and had 6 children and 12 grandchildren combined. They raised their family to be accepting of sexuality and the life choices of others.

Hester and Kirsten were Christian women, but when they would go to church, they felt rejected. Finally, they found a church that would allow them to minister and participate despite their sexuality.

When Kirsten would tell her story, she would say:

"Hester and I have been married for five years and in a relationship for 15 years. Before we met, we were both in abusive heterosexual relationships. My ex-husband would beat me, he took my hard-earned dollars, the money that was supposed to be used to treat my stage 4 cancer, and abandoned me. For Hester, her ex-husband used to physically abuse her and her children. When we met, we vowed to treat one another and our families with love and respect. I treat her children and grandchildren as my own, and she does the same. When Christian people try to tell me that being in a relationship with the one that I love is wrong, I say, "Why would God say that something that feels so bad can be right, and then, when I am treated right and feel good, they say, 'I am wrong?' How can something that feels so good be wrong?""

Common Does Not Mean Right

In his books, The Harbinger and The Mystery of The Shemitah, Rabbi Johnathan Cahn likens America to Israel. America has very close resemblance to Israel: they were founded on biblical principles, the founding father's mandated biblical days as holidays (including the Sabbath for rest), the Bible was the core textbook for school, the Constitution and currency was made with reverence to God, and many more things were implemented to enforce biblical principles within the lives of American people. As a result of the firm stance on God's role in America, the nation prospered more than any other nation in history. People around the world aspire to "The American Dream".

The unfortunate fact is that the blessing associated with being submitted to the promises of God has become the object of affection, and God has been abandoned. The American culture and the culture of all of the nations that follow has become centered on the fruit of holiness rather than its Source. In The Harbinger, Rabbi Johnathan Cahn said:

"The same tolerance that overtook ancient Israel..a tolerance for everything opposed to God, a growing tolerance for immorality and a growing intolerance for the pure-a tolerance that mocked, marginalized and condemned those who remained faithful to the values now being discarded. Innocence was ridiculed and virtue was vilified. Children were taught of sexual immorality in public schools while the Word of God was banned. It was a tolerance that put the profane on public display and removed nativity scenes from public sight..contraband, as if somehow they had become a threat-a strangely intolerant tolerance. "But still, I countered, how does all that compare to what happened in ancient Israel? America doesn't offer its children on altars of sacrifice? "Does it not? he said. Ten years after removing prayer and Scripture from its public schools, the nation legalized the killing of its unborn."

Do not be fooled by what you are commonly seeing! Common does not mean right! Jesus said, "For the pagans run after all these things, and your heavenly Father knows that you need them. But seek first his kingdom and his righteousness, and all these things will be given to you as well. Therefore do not worry about tomorrow, for tomorrow will worry about itself. Each day has enough trouble of its own." God knows your needs and your desires. He hurts when you hurt. He does not choose a painful life for you, but as a culmination of the wrongs done by you, preceding generations, and those appointed in leadership of you, you walk into paths of ignorance believing something is right when it fact, it is wrong. The greatest tool of Satan is ignorance. For this reason, Hosea 4:6 says, "My people are destroyed from lack of knowledge. Because you have rejected knowledge, I also reject you as my priests; because you have ignored the law of your God, I also will ignore your children." When you submit to the will of God, even the things that you feel are going well now will be surpassed. He fills voids inside and out.

If you think that sex can feel good or provide an intimate experience when you are not obedient, you cannot fathom the fruit that can come from walking in obedience to the will of God. Be open to the conviction of God as you read and He reveals to you right and wrong. Feelings can be perverted. You cannot subject your spirit, your destiny, and your potential to your feelings because they can be influenced by spiritual forces of good or bad. Instead, you must subject your spirit, your destiny, and your potential to the words and plans of God. Be fearful of actions that can cause eternal suffering such as sexual immorality because eternity is incomprehensible to mankind. If you've ever had to wait without knowing how long, you can understand the pain in that, but even worse if you were subjected to torture (fire, unending thirst, pain, loneliness, and the feeling of abandonment). Your choices will eventually send you to eternal glory in Heaven or eternal damnation in hell, and your destination is your choice. You make the choice! Your stance towards sex will make or break your truth in that choice. God holds you accountable for words and actions, so when you profess that you are a child of God, but are rebellious when His instructions are laid before you, know that you are equally likely (as someone who never professed salvation) to be in burning sulfur. In James 2:18-20, it says:

"But someone will say, "You have faith; I have deeds." Show me your faith without deeds, and I will show you my faith by my deeds. You believe that there is one God. Good! Even the demons believe that—and shudder.You foolish person, do you want evidence that faith without deeds is useless?"

Your actions towards sex: what you say, what you do, whether you nod your head when someone is telling you something that obviously defies God, or whether you stand up for what the Bible says; all plays a part in where you spend eternity. Sex is a huge global temptation. People are falling prey to the kingdom of darkness persuading them and saying, "It's okay to defy God" everyday. Choose today, will sex be your reason for eternal damnation? Would you prefer never to experience satisfaction again eternally or abide by the laws of God today? Rabbi Cahn said:

"You're only one heartbeat away from eternity. Everything you have—your life, your breath, this moment, it's all borrowed, it's all a gift. And at any moment it all ends with a heartbeat…just one heartbeat, and there's no more time. One heartbeat and the chance to be saved is gone. One heartbeat and there's no more choosing—it's all sealed for eternal life or eternal death."

What The Bible Says About Sex

The Bible clearly states that certain sexual acts are right and some are wrong. God designed our bodies to operate sexually in certain capacities. When we perform sexual acts aside from what has been given to us, we suffer painful consequences. Many people are concerned about the things that the Bible does not directly address, so in later chapters we will discuss them both.

Permissible Does Not Mean Beneficial

Apostle Paul said, "Everything is permissible (allowable and lawful) for me; but not all things are helpful (good for me to do, expedient and profitable when considered with other things). Everything is lawful for me, but I will not become the slave of anything or be brought under its power." (1 Cor. 6:12, AMPLIFIED) Everything that feels good is not necessarily right and helpful, this is also true of sex. Now that we have discussed what the Bible clearly forbids, let's move on.

Summary

- Everything that feels good is not right
- Common does not mean right
- We should look thru the lenses of the Bible for right and wrong
- The Bible has rules for sex
- When sex is performed in a forbidden manner, there are painful consequences

CHAPTER TWO

GET RID OF BAGGAGE!

"Your early experiences dictate your direction: right or wrong."

-Bishop T.D. Jakes

When they had sex for the first time, the hymen was broken and Blake knew that he had married a virgin. He had just gotten married three hours ago. The experience was very intimate for his new wife, Isabel. For Blake, however, he had come from a past of molestation from an early age and promiscuity in his adulthood. His relationship with Isabel was his first attempt to focus his desires on one woman. The first sexual encounter was great for Isabel, but Blake had much more that he desired from sex.

In future instances, when the time for sex would come, he was making requests like, "Hit me", "Scream my name", "flip upside down", "let me put it in your butt", "this time, I want it in your mouth", and the list seemed to expand. Isabel was completely unfamiliar with his requests. Blake was very aggressive with his approach, he would get easily frustrated when she attempted to understand, and sex became uncomfortable for them both. "It seems like you want me to be someone else in the bed, Blake", Isabel would say. "I have had better sex before, that's all. You don't want it in your butt, you don't do it right in your mouth, you pick bad lingerie, your breasts aren't as perky as I like, you don't dance for me how I like it, and you're not that flexible", Blake would say. Isabel would cry profusely saying, "This is not what I saved my virginity for. I wanted a marriage where the man loves me for me! I do not want to live my sexual life imitating other people!"

What The Statistics Say About Sex

Statistics say that 20% of American men and 31% of American women have had one sex partner in their lifetime 56% of American men and 30% of American women have had 5 or more sex partners in their lifetime (Laumann, Gagnon, Michael, Michaels, 1994). While I understand that America is only a small fragment of the world's population, America largely affects the media, the stereotypes, and stigmas of what should be throughout the world. With this in mind, it is no wonder that many people are experiencing sexual dissatisfaction. Most people have someone to compare their spouse to when they have sex. When a comparison is possible, oncoming sex can either cause a hypersensitive reaction (where a person is seeking the experience), or a hyposensitive reaction (where a person is avoiding the experience). In either case, vivid memories are usually attached to sexual experiences, which affects the person's ability to achieve satisfaction going forward. Questions like:

- Why can't you do what he/she did?
- Can't you avoid that because it reminds me of someone else?
- Why can't I remove these flashbacks or memories from my mind?
- How can I find satisfaction in sex again?

And many other questions go unanswered, but become mani-fested in the bedroom as the person attempts to make a new reality with a new partner. The consequence of difficulty attaining satis-faction is running rampant within marriages today; leaving those well preserved disappointed and feeling compared, and leaving those experienced feeling misery because they can never achieve or avoid the inflated memory in their minds.

What The Bible Says About Sex

The Bible gives clear instructions about sex, so that you can have the maximum benefit from the experience. As a result of your choices (or those in authority of you like parents), you can either enjoy sex as a show of love and intimacy for the duration of your life, or you can experience the trauma associated with sexual immorality. Let me be clear that at any point that you choose to align to a biblical standard of sex, it can become a tool of healing, but to submit yourself to the pain that is a sure consequence of sin is your choice.

The Bible clearly says that we are to have sex only in marriage; one man with one woman. (Matthew 19:4-5, 1 Timothy 3:2 and 12) Immoral sex is forbidden. Sexual immorality is defined clearly in scripture as any sexual acts aside from one man and one woman in marriage.

The Bible clearly forbids sexual acts to include: adultery, homo-sexuality (Leviticus 18:22 , Romans 1:26-27), bestiality (Leviticus 18:23 & 20:15-16), prostitution (Leviticus 19:29, Deuteronomy 23:17, Proverbs 23:27, 1 Corinthians 6:15-16), and incest (Leviticus 18:6). In marriage, you render dual authority of your body to your spouse, and you are supposed to meet the wants and needs of your spouse (1 Corinthians 7:3-5). You are supposed to care and nourish your body and your spouse's body physically, emotionally, intellectually, spiritually, and socially. (Ephesians 5:29 and 33, 1 Corinthians 6:19). You should never push your spouse to compromise their beliefs, but instead, seek God, submit your hearts to Him, and allow Him to change them in accordance with His will. (Romans 14:1 & 14 & 23). Regarding sex, one key thing to keep in mind is that you should not be controlled by anything: lust, hatred, sexual desire, selfish ambition, pride, or anything else. (1 Corinthians 6:12 & 10:23) The Bible is clear about some things, and regardless of how you feel, how long ago the Bible addressed the matter, what you have seen, what your family or mentors have done, or anything else, the Bible is the Word of God, and His views towards sex have been unchanged for more than 6000 years. You change and you must use self-control to abide by the laws of God. In everything, seek first the Kingdom!

Learn Right And Wrong

- Adultery - When either partner strays outside of their marriage (in physical or in the mind), by performing sexual acts or desiring someone that they are not in covenant relationship, this is called adultery, and is clearly forbidden in the Bible. (Exodus 20:14, Matthew 5:27). Jesus said: "You have heard that it was said to those of old, 'You shall not commit adultery.' "But I say to you that whoever looks at a woman to lust for her has already committed adultery with her in his heart." (Matthew 5:27-28) That is how serious adultery is. God was very clear when He said in Deuteronomy 5:18 "You shall not commit adultery." The scripture is very plain and very clear. Have respect for marriage. Always be faithful to your partner because God will punish anyone who is immoral or unfaithful in marriage. (Hebrews 13:4, CEV)

- Lust - Every sin as much as adultery begins with lust: "Let no man say when he is tempted, I am tempted of God: for God cannot be tempted with evil, neither tempteth he any man: But every man is tempted, when he is drawn away of his own lust, and enticed. Then when lust hath conceived, it bringeth forth sin: and sin, when it is finished, bringeth forth death. (James 1:13-15, KJV) Lust is the seed that grows a desire for something that is against God. It tells you that you need something that you do not, that when you entertain the object of sin that you will be okay or even feel better, and it feeds many other enticing lies. The Bible describes lust in the beginning saying, "When Eve saw that the tree was good for food, and that it *was* pleasant to the eyes, and a tree to be desired to make *one* wise, she took of the fruit thereof, and did eat, and gave also unto her husband with her; and he did eat." Lust, you know! (See Genesis 3:6)

- Envy - Have you ever wanted something that obviously belonged to someone else? Envy inspires ideas that causes one person to betray another to pervert justice or fulfill a perverted desire with something or someone that is not in their possession or authority. Envy typically walks alongside other fruits of the flesh like lust, sexual immorality, promiscuity, or hatred. Envy inspires actions like theft and adultery.

- Promiscuity - A promiscuous person is one that is not restricted to one sexual partner. One with casual unrestrained sexual behavior; with many sexual partners. It is the breaking of the rule of one man one woman in sexual relations that has caused some of the most damaging experiences for many people. "For this ye know, that no whoremonger, nor unclean person, nor covetous man, who is an idolater, hath any inheritance in the kingdom of Christ and of God." (Ephesians 5:5)

- Orgies are sexual encounters involving many people; an excessive sexual indulgence. God hates it. Sex is not supposed to include other couples or people in your marriage bed. Unrestrained sexual tendency; unrestrained liberty or license to copulate with other couples whether they are your friends or not is forbidden by God. Many people are suggesting that by opening the marriage that they experience added intimacy, but on the contrary, by opening the marriage, you open doors for perversion and the lack of self-control to enter, and these doors are very difficult to close.

- Masturbation and Toys - Within the confines of marriage, the Bible does not say that masturbation or toys are wrong, however, the Bible does show several examples of people who were punished for actions that did not appear to be wrong. The heart is what God judges and your heart while masturbating or using toys can be controlled by forces of good or bad. It is between the husband and the wife to decide whether they would be able to sustain self-control while embracing masturbation and toys as acceptable practices.

Homosexuality is not a political battle, it is a spiritual battle

Beyond what many people see today, homosexuality is a spiritual battle. Homosexuality challenges identity asking, "Why did God send me with this physical gender when I experience different feelings within?". It challenges authority when we say, "I feel like I should be a different gender than I am, and I feel that I was born that way, so I take absolute dominion over my body, and change my physical identity". Homosexuality challenges purpose when a person is confused by whether God made a mistake on their identity, and when they lose focus on what His purpose may have been in the gender that they were assigned physically or genetically at birth.

Gender is an association with physical assignment. As a spirit, you have no genitalia, no sex, and the Bible does not speak about chromosomes being a spiritual matter. Gender is a physical sign of God's assignment for you.

When I was in the military, I signed a contract authorizing my leaders to send me where the country needed me to go. The military leaders from government positions would mandate the number of troops needed to successfully execute certain missions. When tasked, I was given a list of items that I needed to take in order to successfully fulfill my assignment.

Similarly, you are a spirit that has been sent on a temporary mission to the Earth. When God packed your bags (your body), He sent you with all of the equipment that you needed to successfully complete your mission here: talents, family connection, physical ability, location, gender, holy passions, and others. Your responsibility is not to question, "Why did he pack me this bag?", but to find the solution by asking, "With what you've given me, how can I maximize my potential in this life?". You do not have complete insight about your lifespan, and you especially do not see the picture in the large view as He does; having complete awareness of the world from beginning to end. The outrageous fact of today is that nations have allowed people to choose their identity by their feelings. Rather, we were assigned certain attributes for a purpose, and the attributes assigned to us enable our unique purpose and assignment on the Earth. A woman who came to the Earth as a woman has been assigned here for a unique purpose that she cannot carry out if she changes her God-given identity.

Psalms 51:5 says, "Behold, I was brought forth in iniquity, and in sin did my mother conceive me." With this scripture in mind, the attack against each conceived child begins in the womb. For this reason, children are able to be born with birth defects, generational curses, and they can be susceptible to different types of sin as a result of the debt records maintained by the kingdom of darkness. Accordingly, people can be born with genitalia of a man and a woman, they can be born with feelings of insecurity or alternative feelings about their physical gender. Unfortunately, iniquity in the womb or being born gay does not make correct:

- homosexuality
- bestiality
- pedophilia
- sex outside of marriage
- incest
- adultery

- molestation

- rape

- necrophilia

- or any other forms of sexual immorality written in the Bible (See Leviticus 18)

Similar to intellectual property transactions. The kingdom of darkness charges wages for each time you make use of their intellectual property called sin. The Bible gives you details about what sin. 1 John 3:4 says, "Everyone who commits sin is guilty of lawlessness; sin is lawlessness." The law is the Torah, the books written by Moses: Genesis, Exodus, Leviticus, Numbers, and Deuteronomy. The presentation of temptation to break the law is not a biblical reason to break the law. The presentation of a birth defect is not a reason to modify the Bible. Sin is not biblical or an acceptable lifestyle according to the Bible. God did not make mistakes in anyone's conception, neither did He desire for anyone to live with the torment that comes alongside living a life of sin, and sexual immorality is no different.

God has given man and woman immense power and capability

I remember when my husband and I were farming tilapia. We wanted to eat more organically, so we chose to do certain things to develop sustainable sources of organic food. When we studied about the nutrition of the tilapia and things that we could do to ensure that we gave them a healthy diet, we found others who mass produce foods for large populaces. In most instances, male animals grow larger than female. Fish, chicken, beef, and many other animals typically have larger more meatier males than females. As I was learning all of the ways that I can feed the fish to nourish my body organically, I found that others are doing the complete opposite with the same fish! Some food suppliers genetically modify the animals that are in our food supply, so that they can increase in profit. If they are genetically modifying the food, how do you think that would affect the person who ate that food? Possibly genetic abnormalities at birth?

Many times because people are not exploring and gaining wisdom, they face things superficially; creating unbiblical hypothesis such as, "I was born with both genders, therefore God did not choose, and I get to choose". Whereas, God chose a gender for you, but because He created you so powerful, you altered His plan to prosper you in your assigned identity.

In addition to the phenomena of those born with abnormal genitalia, spiritually, male demon spirits can enter females and cause them not to desire males. I have said earlier that there is a demon spirit for every perversion. When evil spirits that inspire lesbianism have taken possession of a woman, they will make her where she does not desire a man. On the contrary, female spirits can enter males, and cause them not to desire females. These are demonic spirits whose chief aims are to inhibit creation and invoke unholy passions in the bodies of people. Open your eyes and be spiritually aware!

When the spirit of a male is inside of a female or vice versa, it is not because God created them that way. God never created these demon spirits to inhabit humans, but because of sin, these things happen. And when it does happen, it does not mean God made it so. Satan is a force in your everyday life. The beauty of the complete biblical testimony is that deliverance is possible. When a person is delivered from demonic possession or oppression, it causes correct godly attraction. Whatever the case is, if anyone is thus taken over by these demons and finds his or herself in these patterns and satanic habits, deliverance in the name of Jesus Christ of Nazareth is available for its correction. There is deliverance for anyone in the name of the Lord.

Let The Past Be The Past!

Past memories should be used for wisdom not comparison. Wisdom enables you to make a brighter future, rather than comparison that keeps you ensnared to the past. Let your future be different than your past. Free yourself and your spouse from the activity of the past! Every relationship is different, and can never be the same. No matter how closely two people may seem, they are not identical, and they can never be the same. So there is no grounds or basis for comparison between two relationships with the exception that you are bound, and need to be free.

Do not request "what a previous boyfriend or girlfriend did", that your spouse look comparable to something or someone else, that they talk like someone else, or anything else. Appreciate your companionship with a unique individual. When you make comparisons, or request that your present relationship carry resemblance to a past relationship, it is demeaning to the person that you are currently with. It does not show appreciation to the God who created a unique identity within each human, and it does not show love for the possibility of the spouse you chose to reach their maximum potential.

Do not request to know "if you are doing better than a previous wife, husband, girlfriend, or boyfriend." I want to charge partners to completely abandon negative comparisons and thoughts of competition between your present and your intimate past (outside of your current marriage).

Be aware of rape or molestation and how it may make your spouse uncomfortable to certain approaches in sex. At times, if your spouse experienced sexual trauma in his or her past, they may present hyposensitive reactions to sex. Even in subliminal circumstances (such as while they are sleeping), they may fight or make a presentation of discomfort about certain sexual approaches. Be mindful. Discuss with your spouse how you can avoid retrieving those triggers. Remember, sex is healing, therefore, your awareness of these triggers as a couple gives you the opportunity to free one another from their hold. Be patient. If your spouse has memories that cause them to avoid or to have additional aggression in approaching sex, pray for them. Speak biblical affirmations for their healthy views of sex. Speak forgiveness affirmations on their behalf. Intercede for them.

Be aware of the effect of sex on those outside of your home. You may need stricter boundaries in some relationships because of a person's temptation for sex with you or because of the person's reservations around you. Sex may have damaged them causing hypersensitivity or hyposensitivity.

Once a person's sexual hopes and wishes have been abused, repressed, or denied over a period of time, it will definitely affect their sexual approach and sensation. Do not bring your past into your marriage bed: unbiblical fantasies, a clothed heart, brokenness, or perceived sensations from a previous partner.

Biblical sex will not feel like an affair

In affairs, you have excitement, secrecy, and adrenaline. In affairs, there is an element of temporary. You know that when you have a dislike, a disagreement, or another interest that the affair can end.

Rather than in marriage, you have vowed to persist thru disagreements, discomfort, sickness, and health. In marriage, you experience ups and downs. In marriages you love to cover over imperfections, and you have a wholesome and committed relationship. As Bishop Jakes said, "There is the difference in the taste of a stolen cookie".

When you attempt to get your spouse to act as an affair, it does not work. They can tell if you are physically with them, but spiritually with someone else. As was the story in Genesis, Jacob laid with Leah, and did not notice that he had been tricked until morning. Genesis 29:25 says, "When morning came, there was Leah! So Jacob said to Laban, "What is this you have done to me? I served you for Rachel, didn't I? Why have you deceived me?".

Referring to the wife within the union of marriage, Bishop Jakes said "She is supposed to be your treasure chest and at different ages, you unlock different treasures." He went further to explain that sex in the covenant of marriage is holy. He said that the hymen was placed within the woman as a veil to be removed. When the penis enters the vagina and breaks the veil, you enter the Holy of Holies; the sanctuary of her body where divine work takes place. Creation takes place in her womb, and anyone who enters that sanctuary will be judged.

You will not have the same worship experience in an affair as you do in a marriage. In the marriage, you have been granted entrance into the sanctuary, and because of the divine covenant, you can enjoy the privilege of being the only one there. The intimacy of marriage cannot be equaled!

Satan uses Abstinence during marriage

The Bible says: "Do not deprive one another except with consent for a time, that you may give yourselves to fasting and prayer; and come together again so that Satan does not tempt you because of your lack of self-control." (1 Corinthians 7:5). You see, the Scriptures are not silent on abstinence; God's word as quoted above is God's rule for it.

Unless mutual agreement between the couple, abstinence during marriage is not supposed to happen. Abstinence during marriage is the ultimate dream of Satan: disunion, disruption, conflict. The Bible says: "don't refuse sex to each other, unless you agree not to have sex for a little while, in order to spend time in prayer." (CEV) Then it says if you do not quickly come together again and resume sexual relations then Satan might have the advantage over you because of your lack of self control. So what does that supposed to mean? It means that Satan seeks prolonged abstinence in marriage so that he can destroy the marriage. So we should never allow prolonged abstinence because the devil through it will edge in on us and trip us.

Sex should be consistent and meet the appetite of both partners. In marriage, the norm is sex; the abnormal is abstinence on the basis of consent for a period of time. And not just sex as it were, but satisfying sex for both partners.

Summary

- Statistics show that many prevailing views about sex are different than the Bible

- The Bible says how sex can be done right and how sex can be done wrong

- Commit to applying biblically aligned views of sex to your life

- Appreciate the gender assignment you have and its role in the fulfillment of your life purpose

- Understand the power that God has given mankind

- Let the past be the past!

CHAPTER THREE

DON'T AWAKEN LOVE UNTIL ITS APPOINTED TIME

"Daughters of Jerusalem, I charge you by the gazelles and by the
does of the field: Do not arouse or awaken love
until it so desires."
-Songs Of Solomon 2:7

The Story Of Linda and Mikel

Linda turned 18. She had planned that when she turned 18,
she would move out of her parents home to another state
to go to college. She was born and raised in church, but
she felt that she saw so much hypocrisy that she said to herself,
"I would not care if I never stepped another foot into a church
building again." She remembered seeing her married Sunday
School teachers approaching her peers in junior high school with
sexual advances. She remembered hearing her Pastor arguing with
his wife across the pulpit and she decided to abandon her home
teaching and find out what life was really about on her own.

She enrolled in college in North Carolina. The atmosphere
offered so many fun activities for people with her interests. She
loved to dance. There were sororities that danced a lot, they had
lots of camaraderie, and it appeared that if she joined, she would
have an ally whenever she needed one. She joined the sorority
and began participating in many activities. She grew a name for

herself and the men were hypnotized by her dancing. She would shake her hips and swing her hair, she was graceful, charming, and sexy at the same time.

She would get approached all the time by men wanting to spend time with her, but she would decline. She had a standard in mind.

In her Sophomore year in college, Linda met Mikel. He was handsome and very fit. His muscles were very toned and his speech was sweet. He would tell her how beautiful she was, and she would chuckle. His words would make her lose track of what she needed to do, where she needed to go, and how she was supposed to get their; she was captivated by him.

When he kissed her for the first time, she could not wait for the next. Then, they went from kissing to petting. As he was heavily touching her, she would imagine him undressing her. In her imagination, if he would take everything a step further, she would enter this dreamland where her body would signal from head to toe, and their relationship would become even more intimate and exciting than before. One day, in his dorm room, Mikel and Linda were kissing and petting, then they began undressing one another. They had intercourse for the first time. For Linda, it was not entirely as expected, it actually hurt and the blood was everywhere. Her friends told her, "It usually hurts the first time, so you have to do it again to get the real sensation."

She and Mikel began having sex every time they would get together. They could not imagine their relationship any other way. It had become habitual to have sex every time they got together. After four months, Linda started having really serious heartburn and she was getting tired all of the time. She took a pregnancy test that came back positive. Mikel was excited.

Linda decided to abandon the night life. She wanted to start getting ready for the baby: planning a baby shower, moving out of the dorm into an apartment, and getting prepared for the baby to have a room. Mikel wanted to transfer to another school, so that he could experience a more vibrant night life. He moved and continued partying while Linda was experiencing different complications in her pregnancy. When the baby was born, Linda would ask for Mikel's help to provide for him, and he would say, "Can't you find that cheaper?" or "If I give you money for that, I will not have money to go into the club tonight." Their relationship ended, but it was very painful for LInda. She had to face an unexpected reality that she was now a single mother.

Sex does not combine will

Sex does not create character: one has it prior and improves it over time. Many people learn the hard lesson that sex does not make good character. In the heat of the moment, when the passion seems abundant, your mind begins to melt in the delight, and you're hypnotized believing that the passion of sexual immorality could last forever. Similar to Linda and Mikel, life circumstances alter your decisions. When Linda found out that she was pregnant, her standard for herself changed. She no longer wanted to enjoy the night life. Instead, she wanted to enjoy preparation for a baby. She wanted to abandon certain forms of entertainment, so that she could devote time to her offspring. Meanwhile, Mikel was also excited about the baby, but he wanted to increase his entertainment. Sex transforms everyone differently.

Your upbringing has affected your views on parenting amongst many other things. Everyone else in the world also has an up-bringing and is affected by whatever that may be. For some, they are striving hard to oppose critical words that condemned their future possibilities, while others are floating on the encourage-ment of others. Some people are experiencing repressed desires for entertainment, and place their life emphasis onto entertain-ment now because of prior restraint, while others are habitually enjoying entertainment. So many scenarios exist in this life. Set standards that do not change with physical circumstance. Look for virtues rather than curves and muscles, and do not attempt to awaken love until you have found a match for the virtues that you desire. Physical attraction can be on your list too, but the spirit and its character is more important. It is love and character that keeps loving relationships together, so keep your eyes open to discover virtue.

Everyone Matures Differently

Everyone matures differently and sex is not a medication to ex-pedite the process. You must assess maturity before you advance the relationship. You must talk and find out the basis for their views.

When my husband and I had first met, there were many differ-ences in our upbringing. I was born and raised In a Suburban area in Ohio. My family always bought our food from the local gro-cery store. We attended church on Wednesdays and Sundays, but I had very few memories of growing spiritually or being connected spiritually or even held accountable to it. My school used paper slips and phone calls for discipline and many children were not intimidated by those methods, so the children were disrespectful many times to the adults.

On the contrary, my husband grew up in a Suburban area of Ghana where they grew and cared for their own food supply. He would attend church overnight, sometime on mountain tops, and was very challenged to be intentional in his spiritual growth. His teachers at school felt accountable for their students. They were permitted to spank them if they ever saw them misbehaving: inside or outside of school. The kids that he grew up around were treated very sternly if a hint of disrespect was shown.

When we were courting, we knew that both of our upbringings were very different, so we started with the hypothesis that both of our upbringings could be wrong, but that we would explore what the Bible says, and create our marriage culture from it. When we catch ourselves saying, "I think this should happen because this is what I have seen before", we hold one another accountable to examining whether the action is aligned with the Bible. In this way, we can know right and wrong rather than making it up. Then, no one feels superior to the other because the Bible is the source of our solutions.

You want to awaken love with a person who loves you enough that they are willing to re-examine their perspectives and compromise for what is best for you. When other differing religions, philosophies, and desires come in, it becomes very difficult to arrive at the same page. Sex does not mature, and it does not change belief systems. Sex is not a medicine to change a person. Common beliefs grounded to the Word of God are pertinent before you awaken love with another person. For this reason, 2 Corinthians 6:14-16 says, "Do not be yoked together with unbelievers.

For what do righteousness and wickedness have in common? Or what fellowship can light have with darkness? What harmony is there between Christ and Belial? Or what does a believer have in common with an unbeliever? What agreement is there between the temple of God and idols? For we are the temple of the living God."

Summary

- Sex does not combine willpower
- Everyone matures differently

CHAPTER FOUR

BE HEALTHY SO YOUR CHILDREN CAN HAVE HEALTHY SEX

"To parents of infants and toddlers, their children's sexual development may seem a long way off. But actually, sexual development begins in a child's very first years. Infants, toddlers, preschoolers, and young school-aged kids develop an emotional and physical foundation for sexuality in many subtle ways as they grow.

Just as they reach important physical and emotional milestones, like learning to walk or recognize mom and dad, young kids hit important milestones in how they recognize, experience, and feel about their bodies, and how they form attachments to others. The attachments established in these early years help set the stage for bonding and intimacy down the line.

By understanding how your kids grow and learn, you can play an important role in fostering their emotional and physical health."

-www.kidshealth.org

The Story Of Octavia

As Octavia reminisced about her childhood, she said:

"I can remember when I was 6-years old. When my mother came home, I was laying in my bed. She said that I had a fever. She kept trying to find out what was wrong with me, but I had no words. I did not know what was my fault or my father's. I was scared for her to be very upset with me. She moved me to my brother's room and changed my bedsheets. As she did it, she found my bloody panties. I could hear her sobbing loudly in my room. "My little girl! Who did this to my little girl?!" I was without words."

At the time of her reminiscing, Octavia had reached her 28th birthday. She was a beautiful woman. Octavia had grown up in a physically and sexually abusive household. Her father would sexually abuse her from the age of six until she was taken away by the state government's child protective services division at age 14. She still would have flashbacks about the incidents she had with her dad. She could remember seeing her siblings treated the same.

At age six, on the first occurence of her rape, she described:

I was sitting with my father watching Bambi on his lap. I could feel something protrude from his pants onto my back, but I was not aware of what it could be. I thought maybe it was the remote or something. Then, he asked me to rub the area, and I did as I had been instructed. Eventually, he pulled something out that looked like a sausage, and began pulling my panties down. I did not know what he was doing, but it was my dad, so I did not feel a reason to panic. Then, he was pushing the thing into me, and it was hurting, so I started to say, "Daddy, it hurts", and he would say, "It won't hurt for long!" I started screaming and crying, but he would not stop. He kept saying, "It will be okay. Just a second longer." Afterwards, I laid in a puddle of blood and sticky wetness. He told me, "Get your mess up before your mother comes and next time, don't make a big mess like that. Your mother won't be happy about that mess!" I hurried to clean the mess up because it was 2:00 PM, and I knew my mother would get home by 2:45 PM. I was in so much pain, but I rushed as fast as I could. My pelvis burned like it was on fire and I began to cry because of the intensity of the pain. My father came and enraged he said, "Move! Let me get this up before your mother gets here. Clean yourself up! Your mother is not going to want to hear all of that crying and whimpering when she comes home from work." I went and laid down in my bed. I took off my bloody panties and put them under my mattress. I felt horrible.

She took me to the hospital, where I had to get stitches from my anus to my vagina; the entire area had been ripped completely. When the doctors removed my mother from the room, a few people came in from the child protective services. They told me that my words would be safe and would be used to ensure my safety, and that this never happened again. I told them exactly what happened.

When I left from the hospital, I left with my mother, and she told me that my father was gone. "If he could do something like that to his own daughter, he does not deserve to be around. He needs to get some help before he can consider coming around the family again".

Six months later, my father said that he had gotten help, and my mother let him move back in. When he came back, everything intensified. He also engaged with my siblings, and my mother tried to ignore it all. Eventually, when I was 14, child protective services removed us from my parents."

When Octavia was an adult, she was a complete avoider of men. Despite her beauty, she would always have flashbacks of her father when she would see men, and she could not sustain attraction.

Make Healthy Sexual Boundaries And Watch Your Generations Prosper

Some of the most disturbed people are parents who watch their children experience hardships. When in their right minds, everyone wants to see their next generation succeed, and sex is a huge factor that can lead your children to success or failure. You must make firm stances on sex, so that you can experience the joys of parenting as they grow older and make healthy relationships and fruitful choices.

Your children will be affected by your views of sex. They will hold high or low esteem to sex in part by how you do. Their views of sex will change as they watch your associations and see the perspectives on sex of the people that you entertain. In addition to your views of sex, your children will watch your body language when other people talk about their sexual views. They will watch you uphold or pervert justice as sexual boundaries are crossed or when they are placed.

Children can be scarred or affirmed by sex and its relationship with you

They can emulate healthy relationships or unhealthy behavior. The people that are most affected by sexual vices and unholy indulgences are always children. Anything that is not corrected in your life can pass on to your children.

For example, in the Bible, King David struggled with sexual temptation. When reading about his life, you will find several instances where he did not abide by the commands of God, but when you read further, you will see the heartache that he experienced as his children took sexual immorality even further. One of his sons raped his daughter, one killed the other for revenge, and a lot of turmoil remained throughout his life as a result.

Sexuality is affecting very young children; even the unborn fetus!

In his video, America The Beautiful 3, Darryl Roberts exposed the changes in legislation, and how governments have changed laws to allow marketers to sexualize the children. Beauty pageants, commercials, internet pop-ups, video streaming, and many other sources of media are teaching your children about body image, eating disorders, pornography, and other sexual matters. Lawyer Michael Brody said, "These marketers are very similar to pedophiles. Okay? They are child experts. If you're going to be a pedophile, or a child marketer, you have to know about children and what children are going to want." Even though you may naively be thinking that media exposure and lack of discretion is okay, there is proof that the sexualization of our children is causing harm. As subliminal as they may be, the exposures are directly correlating with the ages of our youth interest and performance in sex.

CNN broadcasted a case of oral sex performed on the playground by 4-and-5-year olds, the article said:

"The claim, filed by attorney Gregory Owen on behalf of one child, alleges 4- and 5-year-olds at the First Lutheran Child Development Center in Carson, California, were performing oral sex on each other at the preschool.

The suit alleges that in addition to acts performed on the 5-year-old plaintiff, other students were removing their clothing and engaging in sexual acts on the playground and during nap time."

Children are performing acts that they are being exposed to. While they may have been exposed within their home, it is also highly likely that they could have accessed the behavior on the internet, in a magazine, or on TV. Pornography and sexually explicit behavior is common in the media: magazine, newspapers, television, radio discussions, and books are easily accessible for children and expose them to unbiblical views of sexuality.

In an interview of Darryl Roberts on Media Mayhem, he said, "The largest demographic of porn users are young boys ages 11-17". He mentioned that children he had interviewed admitted to exchanging their lunch money for prepaid cards, so that they can buy pornography. Experts say that the average age for a child's first exposure to pornography is 11 and 12 years old, and majority of those children witnessed it involuntarily[2]. Pop-ups, commer-

---

2   http://national.deseretnews.com/article/802/adolescent-addiction-when-pornography-strikes-early.html

cials, and advertising are forcefully exposing our children to things that their brains are not mature enough to comprehend.

In an article on national.deseretnews.com, psychobiology professor, Bertha Madras and Neuroscience professor Peter Kalivas commented about the vulnerability of the youth because of their underdeveloped brain. An excerpt from the article said:

In an interview of young men addicted to porn, he found that the youth become emotionally detached, unable to have a healthy erection, negative feelings and emotions towards the opposite sex, depression, and extreme anxiety about what is supposed to be performed in the bedroom.

Beauty pageants have even lowered their standards; allowing children more body exposure than ever before. Halloween costumes, children's clothing, and modeling agents are teaching children that the exposure of their sexuality gains them awards. Young girls are beginning to wear make-up as early as preschool.

Porn films attempt to portray young girls for men who have erotic fetishes

In her article on cracked.com, Dawn Morrow talked about sexual products that are being marketed and sold to children. Clothing lines such as Abercrombie have incepted thongs with words like, "wink, wink" and "eye candy", push up bras, tramp stamps (temporary tattoos to be placed on the lower back) and other sexually enticing garments made at sizes to fit 7-year olds. Stripper poles are being sold in the toy section, baby dolls called "Hooker dolls" are being sold portraying sex as a profession and the body being exposed, school supplies with Playboy symbols, virgin bikini wax, and so many other items that are being made and marketed to entertain children's sexuality.

Whatever God created is created for time and for seasons

There is a time for everything, including sex. There is a time for children to be rightfully taught and exposed to their sexuality and to the issue of sex. Otherwise the beauty of sex will be misrepresented to the children.

Children are made to love and to respect anything by way of training and upbringing. If you want your children to value and to respect sex, you have to introduce them to this holy act. Children are associating body image and appearance with worth. They are learning that the body should look comparable to what is being broadcasted, they are believing that the behaviors that saturate the media are those that they should portray, and they are being highly affected. You must guard what they are being exposed to, so that they can be preserved, and experience healthy sexuality.

Sex should not be prematurely shown to children

The world does not have the same lens or convictions about right and wrong as you do. Whatever your children are exposed to should be censored. You are responsible for your children and training them the way that they should go!

Apart from the television, parents should have separate rooms from their children where they can be intimate privately. It would amaze you how many children actually see their parents making love when you think that they are sleeping. This is the reason why children should live in separate rooms from their parents even at an early age.

Children's perceptions of sex are damaged by witnessing it prematurely. Children are fast learners and they can also regrettably learn. When a child is raped and abused sexually, the beauty of sex has been obscured from that child forever except when God comes to the child's rescue. The God ordained pleasure and sanctity of sex will forever dissipate from the child's life and physiology unless they submit themselves to God.

Rape damages children

Nothing damages children like rape because they feel unprotected even in their skin. In Maslow's hierarchy of needs, next to physiology (food, water, shelter, etc.) is safety. When a child feels that they cannot find safety in their own skin, it is a psychological attack; they feel the need to continually protect themselves and display guarded, distrusting behavior.

In addition to the potential guarded behavior that can come from a child's exposure to sex prematurely, is hypersensitive behaviors. Treatment centers for addictions are reporting children participating in treatment programs for sexual addictions to include pornography. When a child becomes addicted to sex, they become emotionally detached-not caring about whether the other person is being hurt or treated humanely, they lack the ability to become satisfied, and they have difficulty responding appropriately to a healthy sexual experience. I always believe that the devil goes after great destinies even in their infanthood to taunt them with acts that demoralize and debase. Do you suppose the psychological trauma that a child suffers when raped? It takes the healing balm of the Son of God to completely erase that ordeal and to give the child a new start and a new life altogether.

Lack of modesty damages children

When the child's body is exposed, they become less sensitive in those areas. The areas are more prone to be touched (even in casual and innocent ways), and the exposure creates a more expanded standard of what is appropriate and acceptable. The body parts that you teach your child to cover are the ones that they will have the highest sensitivity about, they will have increased reservations about people touching them in certain places, and their radar will be more sensitive if perverted possibilities were to arise. Teach your child to cover the portions of their body that you know become associated with sexual responses. Between the shoulders and the thighs lie many of the most erogenous zones and as they proceed into their youth, these areas begin sending off pheromones that are attractive to others. Protect them from the possibility of perverted hearts misusing their innocence. Do not allow Satan to creep in and make a residence in the mind of your child!

Summary

- Make healthy sexual boundaries and watch your generations prosper
- Children can be scarred or affirmed by sex and its relationship to you

- Sexuality affects very young children; now even those unborn
- Porn is being made to accommodate fetishes of men or women who desire to see the innocence taken from young girls
- Whatever God creates has a season and a time
- Sex should not be prematurely shown to children
- Rape and lack of modesty can be damaging to children

CHAPTER FIVE

MAKE SEX GOALS

"Excellence is never an accident. It is always the result of high intention, sincere effort, and intelligent execution; it represents the wise choice of many alternatives - choice, not chance, determines your destiny."

— Aristotle

The Story Of Sean and Juliyah

Sean was raised in a small town. His parents made the choice to separate themselves when they had gotten married because their families had different worldviews, and they noticed the consequences that transgressed: some were single parents, some had bad health ailments, some had continuous conflicts in their marriages (adultery, religious differences, and open marriages that had turned into abandoned marriages), and the list goes on. His parents had experienced various situations where they experimented with learned behaviors, and reaped painful consequences, and they vowed to one another, "We are going to do our best with our children. We will teach them right and wrong from a biblical worldview, so that they do not have to experience the same hardships that we did." Sean's parents did not want to raise their children around all of the chaos, so they saved up their money, and moved to a small town in Wisconsin.

Once they settled into their small home, they used their savings to purchase a commercial building, which they used to start Heavenly Manna Supermarket. The supermarket became a staple in the town. They did a lot of kind deeds for those that were distressed in their community and they grew great reputations and loyal relationships with many elite people of their town. Their business prospered and their family was always well supplied.

They homeschooled Sean and his three siblings and exposed them to different lifestyles and worldviews as they saw the children were mature enough to interpret it. When Sean was 23, he met Juliyah at his parents' supermarket. She came in and asked, "How do I apply for a job?" He directed her to his parents where she was hired, and began working as a cashier. Sean and Juliyah began to have interest in one another.

Sean talked to his parents saying, "I really like Juliyah. I think that she could be the one. I want to save everything for marriage even our first kiss, so that it can be very special. How do you think I should tell her this?" His parents were very happy for him. His dad said, "Son, she is a very sweet girl. She has been raised with very similar values as we have raised you. I think that you should be honest with her and tell her how you feel. Once you are both open and honest about your feelings towards one another, it becomes very difficult to avoid kissing, touching, or anything else, so I suggest that you keep someone with you that can hold you both accountable to your purity goals." "I will dad. Thanks for understanding and giving me good advice," Sean said.

While Juliyah was at work, Sean spoke to her parents and said, "Juliyah works at my parent's store. My parents really appreciate her and so do I. I have grown to really like her, and I wanted to ask your permission to begin courtship with her. We will save everything for marriage (even our first kiss), and we will keep accountability partners around so that we are held accountable to our goals. They said, "We are so excited! This is great news! Of course, you can begin courtship with our daughter! We will be praying for you both."

Sean and Juliyah courted for six months, then they got married. Their first kiss was monumental. It was the first time that either of them had shown affection towards anyone in the manner they had. Sex for the first time was breathtaking. They were able to explore and find what one another liked without comparisons. Within their first year of marriage, they were pregnant, and within five years, they had three children. They raised their children with the same values and principles that their parents had taught them.

At age 85, Sean and Juliyah had been best friends and lovers for 62 years. They had 7 children, 28 grandchildren, and 57 great-grandchildren; all products of loving married couples. At age 92, Sean passed away within minutes of Juliyah, their homegoing celebration brought thousands of people together from all across the world. Many people shared memories of their love and their disagreements. Everyone was able to laugh about how they were so affectionate yet they knew how to press one another's buttons. Many people changed their habits because they aspired to live a life of impact as Sean and Juliyah had. From childbirth alone, they had created a community of people that demonstrated love towards others. Thru their travels and their international ministry, they mentored millions. They commonly spoke about love, making good decisions, and leaving a powerful legacy. Sean and Juliyah left their money to a growing foundation to restore biblical marriage and childrearing; which is forecasted to touch 3 million people per year.

Your life is a portrait of your choices

Choose How You Want To Live Your Life. You can make choices that will leave a grand legacy and positively affect many people as Sean and Juliyah did, or you can live a life that regards you as a painful memory whenever someone mentions your name; the choice is yours! Every day, as you are interacting with others, you are making the choice to leave a good or bad memory. As Veronica Roth said in her book, Divergent,"One Choice, decided your friends. One Choice, defines your beliefs. One Choice, determines your loyalties - Forever. ONE CHOICE CAN TRANSFORM YOU".

In addition to making choices about how to treat others, you also have freewill to choose whether or not you will choose the same lifestyle as those that preceded you. You may know how your parents lived. You may know how your grandparents lived. You may have cousins, friends, teachers, mentors, and others that have influenced you. It is your choice to decide which lifestyle choices you will apply to your own life, and you must take self-responsibility for your choices and your life.

Sex choices can propel or deter you from your destination. Even in temporal circumstances, sex connects two individuals into one course. You may decide to relocate or not to relocate simply because of the escalated passion in a relationship. It is wise to be firm with your standards regarding sex.

Freewill is a blessing from God. You have the ability to choose to abide by the laws of the Kingdom of Heaven or to betray them. The topic of sex offers many choices. You choose your partner(s), you choose at what point you will have sex, you choose whether you will satisfy their appetite on an ongoing basis, you choose whether you will expose your children to sex at an early age, and the list goes on. The choices that you make about sex will affect many people whether you have chosen to or not.

Sean's parents saw the consequences of their families' decisions (adultery, abandoned open marriages, and others), and decided that they did not want the same consequences to apply to them and their descendants. They applied biblical principles to their lives, and reaped a different result than others in their families. They chose to place a boundary around their sex life and allow their children to see the product of a monogamous marriage. Do you want to experience the same consequences as your family has? Have you seen their deeds and its fruits? Do you like the deed and the consequence?

In my life, I have been able to see and experience good and bad things in relation to sex. I have been able to analyze good decisions as well as bad decisions. I was able to witness areas where relationship complacency may have come in, ignorance took its toll, and fear demolished opportunities. On the bright side, I was able to witness firm transformational decisions, sacrifices for strong moral values, and advocates of strength and positive change. Regarding sex, I was able to see the effects of monogamous relationships with love and without, extramarital affairs, premarital sex, open marriages, promiscuity, homosexuality, transgender, and other sexual preferences. When I analyzed the good and the bad (regardless of whether others thought bad consequence was good or good consequence was bad), I was able to sieve thru, and choose which consequences I want to live with. Choose to live your maximum potential! Don't settle for mediocrity!

Choose How You Want To Raise Your Children

Your stance on sex will affect generations beyond your own. It will affect families beyond your own. When you have chosen a path for your life, your choice will also affect your parenting, your mentoring, your reputation, and observers. You may find bad habits that exist in your environment that you do not want your children to believe that you condone. You may find language that you do not want to become habitual within your family; these choices are yours! In Proverbs 22:6, the Bible says, "Start children off on the way they should go, and even when they are old they will not turn from it." This scripture tells us that you are accountable for how your children turn out because it is your responsibility to start them out.

Many parents feel that their children have "strayed from their instruction" because they make stances, but do not uproot their children to be in an environment that is 100% conducive to their parenting goals.

Are your children attending schools that are negatively influencing them? Switch them schools! Are your children around people that are negatively influencing them? Stop it! Move! Do something! No excuses! Be radical for the sake of your seed! When you make the firm, sometimes risky decisions necessary to completely re-arrange the environment to be consistent with your values and parenting goals, they will not stray. They will understand the subjects that you have a zero tolerance for. When you say, "I do not agree with that behavior, but...", you are not making a firm stance, and you give the illusion of agreement even when you verbally disagree. As Tiffany Madison said in her book,

Black and White, "If we don't fight for what we 'stand for' with our passionate words and honest actions, do we really 'stand' for anything?". Or, as Jesus said in Matthew 7:16, "By their fruit you will recognize them. Do people pick grapes from thornbushes, or figs from thistles?" Act firmly for the sake of your children, and as Sean's parents witnessed, your legacy will emanate with many, and your descendants will prosper.

Choose Acceptable And Unacceptable Behavior

The world exploits so many different types of sexual behaviors. You must choose which behavior is acceptable and unacceptable. The Bible is God's instruction manual that reveals how you can live fully or die. It tells you how you can experience good sex and how you can be cursed thru sex. Many people inhale and exhale, but they do not live; they have no fulfillment. Many people are distracted by sex raves that cause them to explore biblical evils. When you choose biblically unacceptable behavior, you inherit curses as a consequence of your choices. When you ally with the Bible, the possibilities are endless. It's your choice, will you live a fulfilling life or will inhale and exhale awaiting expiration?

Regarding sex, my parents made radical decisions within our home, but our environment was not consistent with their values. They were married before I was born, and I always saw the product of their love for one another. I knew that they kept sex as a part of their marriage intimacy, and displayed it nowhere else. When males came over, they had stern limits about where they could go if there were females in the house. We were taught about appropriate and inappropriate touching: do not touch one another between shoulder and thighs. Despite my parents very clear rules, there were still others in our environment that were consistently adulterous, dressed provocatively, exploited sex with their music and songs, and out of curiosity, I decided to explore.

At age 18, I entered into my first sexual relationship. I was pregnant soon after and after discovering that we both had different values and maturity levels, the relationship resolved, and I was a single parent. I quickly learned the importance of sexual purity and the consequences of premarital sex.

Set The Standard For Those Who You Will Invest Your Time

Everyone has a perspective about sex. They may think that their views are passive or inclusive, open-minded or conservative; whatever their stance, it exists! When you have set standards for what you consider acceptable sexual behavior and acceptable behavior for your family, you must surround yourself with people that advocate for the same views.

In parenting, many times, investing our time in the right people can be the part of the equation that many people miss. Your children learn from you and those that you bring around them. You are influenced by the things that you intentionally put into your mind as well as the behaviors and habits of those around you. Their perspectives on sex may or may not be firm, but if you invest a lot of time with them, you are submitting to their influence.

For Married People: Set Marriage Goals

Your spouse has a sexual appetite. You need to sync to the same sexual rhythm. He or she has desires, things that they would like to explore, sensations that may be untapped. You must make goals to invest time in improving your sexual experience. Sex should not be on the backburner. It is a byproduct of love, marriage, and a desire for closeness, so make sex goals! How many hours per day can you invest into enhancing your sexual experience? How often does your spouse desire sex? What obstacles do you have that limit you from being able to satisfy your spouse, and how can you remove them?

When I was balancing full-time work, full-time school, parenting, and marriage, it was very tiring! I would stay up late working on homework. I had book ideas that I felt overwhelmed about, and I was miserable about not having enough time to express my creativity. I had homework that I had to oversee with my son. There were so many obligations that I was balancing, and sex seemed to be last on my agenda. I decided that I wanted to put more effort into strengthening my marriage, so making sex goals was one such milestone that positively affected my marriage.

Be Firm

There is a time to be firm and a time to be flexible. Being that sex is such an exploited topic, it is very necessary to be firm about this topic. The statistics of those that are tempted by sex are rising as the ages for such desires continues to lower. With the same passion and fervor that you use to pursue your dream, you must also be firm about the acceptable confines of sex.

Summary

- Your life is a portrait of your choices
- Choose how you want to raise your children
- Choose acceptable and unacceptable behaviors
- Set the standard for those who you will invest your time
- For married people: Set marriage goals

CHAPTER SIX

IDENTIFY HOLY AND UNHOLY MATRIMONY

"Soul ties. The thing that can make you hear an old-school slow jam and think of somebody you haven't seen in years. Soul ties. The thing that makes old people who've been together for years finish each other's sentences. Don't you wish mama had told you when you were young that, when you lie with someone, you lie not just with her body but also with her soul? And whatever condition the other person's soul is in, you are guaranteed to take a piece with you—whether you want to or not.."

— Kirk Franklin (The Blueprint)

The Story Of Ajani and Zesiro

Ajani and Zesiro were born and raised in the same neighborhood in Togo. Their families had common values, and encouraged their relationship. They were best friends until adulthood.

Ajani befriended a young man from Azerbaijan named, Kojo. He had different values. His parents did not condone the behaviors that his new friend was suggesting, but they said, "He is old enough to make decisions on his own", so they did not speak about it. Ajani began traveling to visit his friend. He was introduced to different women. Kojo would say, "Man, it's no good to be a virgin. If and when you meet your wife, you won't know how to please her! You have to get warmed up." Ajani took Kojo's advice and began to entertain women.

They began going dancing at local clubs and attracting women with their dance moves. They would take the women home and Ajani had sex for the first time. His first sexual encounter was a means to prove his manhood, he wanted to feel the satisfaction that was long forecasted by Kojo and many others. His first sexual experience was an instant sensation, but because he had not developed a relationship with the woman, it only allowed him minutes of pleasure.

After his first encounter, he was tormented with dreams that he did not understand. He saw snakes at times. In his sleep, he saw a woman that professed to be his wife. He would have sex with her every night in his dream. When he would awake, he would notice that he had ejaculated and fluid had completely soaked his bed.

He would go on rampages for sex; attempting to prove that "He was the man" to every woman that he would have sex with. The snakes in his dream had introduced different dance moves to him that would entice the women to go home with him. He would have sex with them and leave them, but they desired more, so they were instantly transformed by their hypersensitive recollections.

Ajani wanted to increase his pleasure from sex, so he tried orgies, drugs, he added tattoos for increased attraction, and other things that others boasted would add more to his experience, but after ejaculation, the pleasure subsided.

One night, when they were out dancing, a woman rushed over to Kojo and Ajani screaming, "You gave me Aids! I want to kill you!" Ajani was shocked. He had no idea that Kojo had a sexually transmitted disease. He and Kojo left the club. When they left, he said, "Man. Why didn't you tell me? We have been sharing the same women, and I didn't know that you had an STD? I thought we were better than that! Now I could be dealing with something that is terminal!" Ajani was infuriated. He packed his bags to leave for Togo.

Meanwhile, Zesiro was growing a relationship with a lady that he met at a local prayer meeting. They vowed that they would keep sex for marriage. Their relationship seemed to be growing sweeter with each encounter. They would always meet at public places, they would bring accountability partners, and they really enjoyed one another. Zesiro decided to distance himself from Ajani and others that made alternate sexual standards because he was not in agreement with the things that they were doing. He was very careful about his media intake and the music that he listened to. He only entertained music that was consistent with his views about women, sex, love, and presented modesty. When it was time for them to get married, they were as cheerful as a child on Christmas. Their love was so infectious that it made everyone smile and cheer. When they experienced sex for the first time, they were so sensitive to one another's nakedness, their words, their touch, and the experience was breathtaking. Their love increased after their first sexual experience because they understood the immeasurable depths of their love for one another. The words that they would say to one another, they would say to no one else. The way that they would touch one another, they would touch no one else, and the way that they could make one another feel together, they could not find anywhere else.

Three spirits become one

It would be important to refresh our memories as to the fact that God, being spirit created humans in his image and likeness. That means that we too are spirits. So in whatever we do with our lives, our spirit personalities are directly involved. This is especially true in the area of sex.

The most spiritual thing in the world is sex. It is more than just two bodies infusing into each other, it is more than two souls tied together (soul tie); it is actually eternal spirits coming in contact and fusing with other eternal spirits. It is spirit touching spirit; it is a joining of spirits in holy or unholy matrimony.

And in the case of the believer, it is the fusion of God, the man and the wife-all three spirits; the three stranded rope that is not quickly snapped.

In God-ordained sex: husband, wife, God

Since the art of sex is spiritual and God is the creator of everything, He also created sex. When sex is thus engaged, in God's ordained way, it is His spirit, the man's and the woman's that come together. Such a holy matrimony! The idea is this: In a marriage setting, God who is the source and originator of marriage is involved from start to finish with everything there is to it. Two lives pouring into each other, with God in them. As they share their life blood which each other, they share the God in them with each other. It is the most sacred thing in the world.

Zesiro was experiencing the holy matrimony of the three strands merging: he, his wife, and God. The union of the three spirits in holy matrimony is not comparable in sensation or ful-fillment otherwise.

You know embedded in human blood is the spirit of man; that was why He said to Cain: "the voice of your brother's blood is crying out to me from the ground." In the blood is a voice, the voice of the human spirit. A person can bleed to death, you know! As he loses his blood, he loses his life. In the act of sex, two life bloods with the nature and the spirit of God; two doses of holy, God-given breath come together. Is it any wonder that another life usually results from this?

As kissing takes place, body fluids mix, breath is shared, and messages are communicated beyond words. This introduction to sexual contact is serious! At this point, access is being granted in spiritual realms.

A person that is saved is a member of the body of Christ, his or her body belongs to the Lord and the Lord belongs to Him. So when such people come together in the holy act of sex, their bodies and the body of the Lord are joined together in one. In sex, God joins His body with our bodies, and this is called holy matrimony.

Many popular opinions in primitive culture and Christianity believe that God turns His face every time a man and his wife want to have sexual intercourse. People somehow believe that sex is so dirty that God has to turn His face away every time any of His children want to indulge in it. They feel God hates it. How could He hate what He created? Sex is not dirty, it is the holiest thing in the world and God not only enjoins it but joins Himself to His holy children who enter into this holy act in a legally God ordained way.

In perverted sex: husband, wife, Kingdom of Darkness representative

Just as in the case of the legally, God-ordained sex in marriage, so also is the perverted Satan motivated sex outside of marriage. In perverted sex, the spirit of the man or woman who are unregenerate blend into each other with that of the devil at the centre. The three spirits flow together and into one another. Did you ever wonder why 68% of demonic possession comes through sex? Demons spirits (the motivation of those sexual perversions) flow freely from one person to another during the process. Spirits are communicated and transferred through sex.

The source of sin, sickness, disease, infirmity, trial, and tribulation is the kingdom of darkness. While it is true that they prey on our choices, when we accept ulterior views of sex, we welcome everything that they bring. Kojo was being used to advise Ajani away from the biblical laws. A spirit was influencing him to behave in the way that he had, and rather than Ajani standing firm, and influencing him in a positive way, he was tempted to submit to the kingdom of darkness. As a result of his actions, his spirit also became merged with demonic forces: spirits of lust, pride, and infirmity had taken possession of different parts of his body. He no longer had clear thoughts about how he wanted to give and receive sexual pleasure; rather, his thoughts were entirely influenced by a desire for affirmation or approval.

Just like God is actively involved in holy sex by His holy children so also Satan is actively involved in an unholy passion with his own children. A demon or a representative of the kingdom of darkness is joined in bodily form to the persons who are perverted and are indulging the sex act. I would like to mention that demons have passions, I mean evil unholy perverted and degrading passions that are so anti human and when people are thus indulge in those passion and act, you can be sure that they are not the ones doing those things but the devil that is in them. The same way the two who are holy plus God become one flesh; the devil and the persons involved in unbiblical practices also become one flesh; the three shall become one sinful flesh.

Satan commonly uses sex for entrance

There are some demonic ceremonies and initiations that are only done on the ground of sex. If you are a virgin, the kingdom of darkness will not employ you. They require a catalyst to interrupt the mind, and a body fluid to seal the covenant. They use alcohol, enticing motions, mysterious symbols, sharing of food and drinks, childbirth, medications and other sly ways of sharing blood, body fluids, creating fog in the mind and blurring the thoughts. When they have access to a person (because the person trusts the moment and believes that what is taking place is good for them), they take possession of the body, and seal the covenant with tattoos, piercings, surgical procedures, and other sources of blood emission (including sex). They must implore one to go have sex and break his or her virginity before one can be fully integrated into their kingdom. This is a fact of the kingdom of darkness. Similar to the agreements sealed by the king with the signet ring, their receipt of your blood becomes the stamp that authorizes them access to control the thoughts of your mind and the situations of your life.

So in perverted sex, Satan and his demon spirits not only officiate the scene, they actually blend into it and a union of three strands that cannot easily be broken is also formed in the negative. Satan understands the power and the sanctity of sex within marriage and he knows that God is its foundation; so as it is consistent with his nature he would do everything to desecrate it by perverting it. He is so adept at profanity.

Ajani participated in the sexual ceremony. When he partook of the sexual ceremony, he merged himself with demonic forces. Spirits that encouraged him to think about what he can take, what he can prove, and spirits of shame that come along with the possibility of a sexually transmitted disease. His choices affected many more people than originally partook in the sex. Onlookers, his family, his friends, the lady that he slept with, and those observing her. Many people were affected by his choice. His behavior transformed from a focused and driven man to a wandering man; outsourcing his internal voids.

Three bodies become one

You see, sex is an awesome mystery. It encompasses both the spiritual and the physical. Sex is spiritual, yet physical. The mode of expression is the physical organs. It is with these physical organs that the spiritual are always expressed, such is the harmony that God created between the body and the spirit.

We as spirit beings need our physical bodies to operate and to seek expression, even in sex. For he has said at the beginning: "Therefore a man shall leave his father and mother and be joined to his wife, and they shall become one flesh." (Genesis 2:24)

God is the third strand in sex. We noted earlier that sex (holy legalized sex in the context of marriage) involves the man, his wife and God. God being the third party in the act (though not physically seen), He is present. You see, sex is an expression of the nature of God. He created us in His image and likeness, with the ability to procreate like Himself at the same time having pleasure. He created everything plus sex, all for his pleasure and they all came from Him. Sex is a vital part of the nature of God portrayed in his creatures.

He makes sex a permanently enjoyable process (on Earth). It is important that we know that sex is not just only for procreation but for pleasurable intimacy between a husband and a wife, and that to be enjoyed only on the earth. The Scripture states unequivocally clear that marriage which is where sex is to be expressed is only in this life on earth and not in the one to come or in heaven. So it is a blessedness reserved only for the inhabitants of the earth as long as they live. This is so because as spirit beings, we need our bodies for all forms of expression, but when we are no longer in our bodies, the things that the body only does and enjoys will not be there in the spirit world for the spirit to engage in.

God is not engaged in perverted sex; therefore it does not have the same capacity for enjoyment and fulfillment. God is holy, and everything He does is holy. I said earlier that sex is a part of the nature of God. It came from Him; it is an extension of His person and nature. If that is correct and God is holy, you can be sure that He will never indulge or enjoy unholy sex and perversion. So whatever is not pleasurable to the source (God), should never and not be pleasurable to the extension (humans).

Anything that you insert into your body can be used to initiate

What you see, what you hear, what you taste, what you touch, and what you smell can be sources of initiation into the kingdom of darkness. Your senses are portals that can be used a receptacles of temptation.

The kingdom of darkness uses blood to seal covenants into his kingdom. Covenants can be sealed in physical or spiritual. Tattoos, piercings, sexual intercourse, food intake, medication intake, media and music intake, scents, and others sources of enticement can be used to lure people into evil acts.

Thru dreams, audible voices, men and women that are their employed representatives, trances, circumstances, and artistic expressions, the kingdom of darkness sends messages. They network with you, send directions of how to persuade and add others into their kingdom of evil, they initiate sexual dreams, they inflate sinful experiences; giving the mental illusions of increased sensation than is actually possible thru sinful behavior. As a result, many people tormented by dark thoughts become either hypersensitive (seeking) to the things of evil and hyposensitive (avoiding) to the things of God.

The kingdom of darkness preys on the most vulnerable times; when people are at their lowest lows. When the woman has been waiting a long time to bear children (as Sarah submitted to in Genesis), when women dance beautifully (like Samson submitted to in Judges), when you have fasted and prayed but have yet to receive your breakthrough (as Satan tempted Jesus in Matthew), and when people feel emptiness or torment in their body (as the woman with the issue of blood). It is at these times that people are receptive to chemical input in their bodies, claims that witchcraft might work, claims that puncturing their body could relieve ailments or aid in attraction, thoughts that physical image should be changed or modified, and all these things create gates of entrance for demonic forces.

The kingdom of darkness also uses the movement of the body to attract others to sexual behavior. When they have possessed a person, they use the movement of the body to act as hypnotic to others: dances, animal-like movements, hand signals, erotic attire, and appeal. You must be careful of the sexual vices that you allow to enter into your senses because they can be used for good or bad. Sex is one of the prevailing tools used to enter into the kingdom of darkness, so guard it. It is the tool of creation and matrimony. It is used to align with good or evil, so be careful! Use sex to increase your love rather than invoke evil. Seek knowledge rather than submitting to your immediate desire. Stay as a seeker of the Kingdom of God and He will add everything unto you.

CHAPTER SEVEN

IDENTIFY THE FRUIT OF UNBIBLICAL MATRIMONY

"So I say, walk by the Spirit, and you will not gratify the desires of the flesh. For the flesh desires what is contrary to the Spirit, and the Spirit what is contrary to the flesh. They are in conflict with each other, so that you are not to do whatever you want. But if you are led by the Spirit, you are not under the law.

The acts of the flesh are obvious: sexual immorality, impurity and debauchery; idolatry and witchcraft; hatred, discord, jealousy, fits of rage, selfish ambition, dissensions, factions and envy; drunkenness, orgies, and the like. I warn you, as I did before, that those who live like this will not inherit the kingdom of God.

But the fruit of the Spirit is love, joy, peace, forbearance, kindness, goodness, faithfulness, gentleness and self-control. Against such things there is no law."

-Galatians 5:16-23

The Story Of Ailana and Ilyana

Ailana and Ilyana were friends until death. They had been best friends for 15 years, and they believed that they have been a refuge for one another on many occasions.

Ailana was born and raised in a wealthy neighborhood. Her dad was a banker on Wall Street and her mom was a stay at home mom. Despite their prestige, Ailana's home had a lot of conflict. Her dad worked alot, and rather than coming home to build his relationship with her mother, he was a frequent supporter of local prostitutes. Her mom held a lot of resentment towards her dad, so they never got along. Her mom and dad were emotionally detached because of their inner voids, so Ailana did not receive much love from them.

On the other hand, Ilyana was raised in a poor neighborhood. She never quite understood what her parents did for a living, but she saw lots of money exchange hands. She witnessed a lot of drugs and violence. Many people would go in and out of their apartment in the projects, and her parents were in and out of jail. Her parents stayed so occupied with their life of drugs and wild parties, so Ilyana was always left alone.

In the second grade, at a summer cheerleading competition, Ailana and Ilyana met. They had so many things in common, so they exchanged phone numbers and stayed in contact. They remained friends from that day on.

When Ailana turned 18, her parents said, "If you don't find a job, you'll be out on the streets. Desperate for a solution, Ailana would view the internet daily looking for a job. One day, she stumbled upon an ad that said, "$20,000-$30,000 per month for modeling". Excited, she responded to the add and scheduled an interview.

When Ilyana turned 18, her dad said, "I have a job for you. Wear this, ride with your mom and I, and she will show you what to do." She did as her dad told her to do, and everything turned out as he forecasted.

15 years later, Ailana and Ilyana were still best friends. They would laugh and cry together. They would console one another. They still worked the jobs that they began at age 18. Ailana was a porn star and Ilyana was a "high-end escort". In their professions, they had been raped on countless occasions, beat, spit on, they had inserted many foreign objects into themselves to fulfill the fantasies of their clients. Their motto was, "It's all for the money." They only knew two possibilities: selling their bodies or getting a job, and getting a job seemed much less lucrative to them. As a result of their longevity in their careers, they both had anal damage, countless infections (in the eyes, throat, and vaginal areas), they had amassed hundred of thousands of dollars worth of debt for medical bills, and they both had incurable sexually transmitted diseases. Their reputations were connected with their employment, and they answered to the terms, "bitch", "ho", and "whore". They were both addicted to cocaine and alcohol, and they say, "We cannot complete our jobs if we don't use drugs". After 15 years in the business, they lived every day with regrets and repressed desires. They wanted a family, children, the ability to travel, a good reputation, and many other things, but they had practiced their lifestyle so long that they do not know how to achieve it. After 15 years on the job, Ailana was murdered, and Ilyana committed suicide.

The Fruit of Unholy Matrimony

The porn industry alone is said to earn between $2.6 billion and $3.9 billion every year. This means that the porn industry surpasses google, Microsoft, Netflix and combined in annual earnings. Sex is highly exploited, and with the average scene exposing women and men moaning, with faces that appear euphoric, and garments that reveal the beauty of God's handiwork, people are enticed into the illusion that they are adding something to their lives by making unbiblical sexual choices.

Sex does not fill internal voids

Like Ailana and Ilyana some people use the intimate nature of sex attempting to cover childhood voids. When relationships are entered out of a feeling of emptiness, addictions commonly emanate. You will continually search for the emptiness to be filled, only to find that outsourcing the fulfillment does not work. Jesus knocks on your heart; seeking to fill the voids internally in a way that only He can. Sex can offer temporal fulfillment because you experience the closeness of another spirit, but the Bible tells us that Jesus stays closer than a brother when you invite Him. The companionship that you can temporarily enjoy in sex is offered eternally thru salvation in Jesus.

Understanding that sex is a ceremony where spirits are merged (spirits of light or spirits of darkness), it is wise to be clear about which you want connection to. The kingdom of darkness does not play fair. When you open the door and allow entrance, they come in numbers. For this reason, the Bible gives several examples of people such as Mary Magdalene who were possessed by several demons. When several demons are tormenting you, plaguing your every thought, and feeding you with poisonous antidotes to your success, it is very difficult to succeed. Sex is a prevailing tool used by the kingdom of darkness to initiate the loss of full thought, body, and action control. Do not submit to evil sexual practices and relinquish control of your destiny. Maintain a biblical standard for the sake of your destiny, the world that needs it, and the descendants that can take your offering to the next level.

God said to Adam and to Eve: Genesis 2:16-17 "Of every tree of the garden you may freely eat; "but of the tree of the knowledge of good and evil you shall not eat, for in the day that you eat of it you shall surely die." Bishop Jakes said that the sin of Adam was not that he was deceived, it was that he would die for the gift, and betray the giver. Adam made a conscious decision that he loved the woman so much that he would be willing to die for his sin rather than part with her, so he chose disobedience. He was not deceived as she was.

In the midst of temptation, the sensation captures the mind so much that you are deceived, and for some, they sell their birthright to eternal glory. We are spirits with an eternal destiny, but when you lose focus of eternity, and get captured into "right now" pleasure, you have to reap the consequences.

Most people do not discuss the consequences that come from sexual misconduct, but they are treacherous. Some consequences are attacks against your self-image, some are against your generations, and some are against your physical property or your body.

The Internal Fruits of Sexual Immorality

God created muscles in our necks to hold our heads up, but the sin of sexual immorality strips one of that dignity, causes postures to change, heads to bow, and replaces confidence with shame. You think that everybody knows what you have done and negative thoughts fill your heart. When a person is carrying the weight of shame, they are attempting to hide their reality, so they tend to submit to further negative circumstances just to cover up what they have done, and an endless cycle is created. The Webster's 1828 dictionary defines shame as, "A painful sensation excited by a consciousness of guilt, or of having done something which injures reputation; or by of that which nature or modesty prompts us to conceal." Regarding shame, King David said, "My confusion is continually before me, and the shame of my face hath covered me". (Psalm 44:15)

Guilt acts as a chain that ties a person to their deed. When guilt plagues a person, the kingdom of darkness is active reminding them of their deed, planting the idea that there is no way out, and making them feel that the deed is a reflection of who they are.

Shame and guilt cause secrecy. Many times, when a person feels that they have performed something that is wrong, they attempt to cover the wrong with more wrong. Drug addictions, staying distracted, partying, and other things are used to turn attention away from the past. Running from the past can only continue for so long, but guilt and shame make people think that running from the past is necessary.

Physical Consequence To Sexual Immorality

- Sexual disease. Exodus 15:26 says:

  "If you listen carefully to the Lord your God and do what is right in his eyes, if you pay attention to his commands and keep all his decrees, I will not bring on you any of the diseases I brought on the Egyptians, for I am the Lord, who heals you."

When you disobey God with your sexual choices, disease is a byproduct. Disease is not something that everyone gets for sexual immorality, but it is highly prevalent. Reporting on the US, the 2013 statistics from the Center For Disease Control said, " Nearly 20 million new sexually transmitted infections occur every year in this country, half among young people ages 15–24, accounting for almost $16 billion in health care costs." With the statistics in mind, we know that God is still using disease as a consequence for immorality. Submit your sexual choices to God, and you will avoid the shame, guilt, and physical trauma of sexually transmitted diseases.

• Single parenthood. While children are always a blessing, having a child outside of marriage was not the intended design. Neither man nor woman was made complete. Sex is the act that identifies man's need for woman, and woman's need for man. Neither, man nor woman can create without one another, which shows their partiality apart. When a child is raised in a fragmented home (where one of the parents is absent), they are not able to have the equal balance of building feminine and masculine understanding, and developing the entirety of their identity. In Sara McLanahan's book, Growing up with a Single Parent, she says, "It is revealed that children whose parents live apart are twice as likely to drop out of high school as those in two-parent families, one and a half times as likely to be idle in young adulthood, and twice as likely to become single parents themselves." Without the intervention of God, even the most achieved single parents will raise broken children.

- Injuries. The Washington Post reported that injuries related to sex toys doubled since 2007. Many people are desiring to explore sexuality, so of the increase in injuries, 83% were "foreign body removals".[3] The body was designed for sex to be a ceremony of unity, but when it is performed aside from biblical guidelines, hatred, lust, and fits of rage dominate the circumstance. When the heart is motivated by lust and fetishes or foreign objects are used to satisfy the unholy desire, injuries have high probability. Although the sex industry portrays foreign objects being used to increase desire, majority of the examples are actors or actresses in video footage, words within a book, erotic audio, and other forms of entertainment that inflate reality. The reality of the sex industry is that many broken people who love money make their lives vulnerable and submit themselves to the consequences foretold in the Bible. Do not be deceived by the acting or the fancy verbiage. Submit your sexual choices to God, and you will be able to experience maximum satisfaction. "Good understanding giveth favour: but the way of transgressors *is* hard. (Proverbs 13:15)

Summary

- The fruit of unholy matrimony has long-term effects
- Sex does not fill internal voids
- There are internal and external fruits of unholy matrimony

---

3 http://www.washingtonpost.com/blogs/wonkblog/wp/2015/02/10/sex-toy-injuries-surged-after-fifty-shades-of-grey-was-published/

CHAPTER EIGHT

LEARN THE ART OF SPIRITUAL WARFARE

"With the weapons that God has made available to you, he expects you to capture and hold captive every thought and idea that comes into your mind, and to examine these against the backdrop of the Word of God. Those thoughts that are in line with God's will and purpose for your life are to be released and allowed to move freely within your mind. However, those thoughts and ideas that are contrary to the Word of God are to be held perpetually captive and cast out of your mind in the name of Jesus!"
— Pedro Okoro (Crushing the Devil: Your Guide to Spiritual Warfare and Victory in Christ)

The Story Of Ryan and his daughter

Speaking to his pastor, Ryan said, "I remember my little girl, but she doesn't act like my little girl anymore. She used to be daddy's little girl until she reached her teens, and she started really getting into boys. When she was 14, I started hearing disgusting stories about how she snuck over a friends' house with a boy, and lost her virginity in the bathtub. The parents were furious with us and everyone else involved, and I don't blame them. I was disgusted with my own daughter! I cannot believe that she would do that and since, it has only gotten worse. I hear stories about her all of the time. Sex for her is like a drug. She does whatever she can do for sex. I have tried talking to her about it, but I have not done anything yet that has changed her behavior towards sex. She describes the hyperinflated memories; causing her to persistently seek sex in effort to supercede the sensation that she received before. My daughter has not been the same since she had sex."

"Do you pray for her?" said Pastor O'Connell.

"I don't know where to start," said Ryan.

"Bring her here! We will cast every demon out and cancel every contract giving them authority".

Ryan brought his daughter, Melanie, to the pastor. When she entered his office, she began to speak angrily, "Why are you two wasting my time? I can have sex with whomever I choose, wherever I choose. Let me go!"

"Your father knows the little girl that you were. He knows your dreams and aspirations. He knows that you wanted to go to school, but you have become distracted by sex. He knows that you wanted to be very successful, but now you are on the brink of poverty. He brought you here to take back your dreams. Do you want your dreams back?" Pastor O'Connell asked.

"Yes" said Melanie.

"Jesus died, so that you can be free of torment, he paid the price for sin, and you do not need to affiliate with this sin for your success. If you are ready to be freed from this, lift your hands." Pastor O'Connell placed his hands on Melanie's head and said:

"Father, you have given authority to your son to drive out

demons with the blood of Jesus Christ. I break all ungodly oaths, covenants, and pledges that have been made by Melanie or her ancestors. I cancel all plans of the enemy with the blood of Jesus Christ. You evil spirits that torment and direct her into evil paths. Your time with her has ceased. I command you to leave and let her go!" Melanie's spirit lifted out of her body, and her body fell to the ground. Pastor O'Connell continued to pray, saying:

"I sanctify her body and call her free to walk into her destiny in Jesus name I pray. Amen."

When the prayer was complete, Melanie gathered herself from the ground. She looked around, shocked that she had fallen unknowingly. She said, "I feel so light!"

Pastor O'Connell said, "Jesus has delivered you from the torment of the kingdom of darkness. You are free. Go and please God".

Freedom Requires Courage

Freedom requires that you face your bondage and overcome it. You cannot stay in secret to be free. You cannot hide your faults or your vulnerabilities. In John 8:32, the Bible says, "The truth will set you free". Note that the scripture tells you that a secret cannot set you free. Many times, we are deceived by the kingdom of darkness into believing that by concealing or making a truth a secret that we can be free. This lie is far from the truth! Face the truth and be free!

There are times when you may not know what to do. In the times, when you have no ideas, call for reinforcements! As Ryan did, he consulted with a pastor who was familiar with how to fight in spiritual warfare. Pastor O'Connell had developed a relationship with the Holy Spirit, and was able to cast demons out. When spiritual warfare battles become very intense, seek men of God.

You may have seen things that you weren't supposed to see. You may have heard things that you weren't supposed to hear. You may have touched things that you were not supposed to touch. When you did, you created doors and windows of entry because of your choices. The kingdom of darkness has been granted access by your choices. Bishop T.D. Jakes said, "The dangerous thing about the enemy being put out of your house is that he knows where your doors and windows are." Your doors and windows are around your experiences: your rape, your molestation, your sexual experiences, pornography, and so on. You must find a place where you can be honest with people who are aligned with the Kingdom of Heaven, void of the idea of condemnation, and willing to pray with you thru your circumstance. We all experience struggles and no one should make you feel bad about it when you are opening the door for your liberty. Find backup because the kingdom of darkness does not play fair.

Spiritual warfare is continual

In addition to spiritual warfare, you need to build self-control. You can deal with repressed sexuality or from restraining yourself after previous sexual liberty; either circumstance requires extensive growth in self-control. Your self-control muscle grows from transferring your focus on temptation or your struggle to righteousness. You may be saying to yourself, "How do I overcome this temptation?", and the answer is, "Focus on righteousness".

Increase your prayer time, increase your Bible intake, commune with other God-seekers, invest in your relationship with the Holy Spirit. The more intimate your relationship becomes with God, the less strength temptations will have on you.

The enemy continually attempts to come back. The longer you walk with God, the lesser frequencies that you have potent tempting experiences. You develop self-control to defeat the enemy: you go from savoring sexual sin to participating but feeling guilty, then you learn to make solutions that allow you safeguards around sin.

"Your spirit is saved, but the body is not", said Bishop T.D. Jakes

Your body is stimulated by nerve endings, your senses, your emotions, messages transmitted from the brain throughout. Sensations are transmitted throughout the body regardless of how holy you perceive yourself to be. Temptation is a part of being a mortal being in a fleshly body. It is a continual battle. You clothe your body, you set proximity boundaries, and you guard your sensory portals to prevent temptation. Most importantly, you develop self control to overtake temptation.

Sometimes you must get free from your past, so that you do not bring home memories and practices of the past. Anything absent of the Spirit needs to be controlled. The thoughts and the body need to be controlled. Exercise! When your flesh and the kingdom of darkness is used to having authority over your mind, and you choose to take it back, it is a battle. You must replace unbiblical thoughts with biblical thoughts. You must replace self doubt with affirmations of an overcomer. You must change your speech to concur with victory, and by repetition your faith will increase. For this reason, Romans 10:13 says, "Consequently, faith comes from hearing the message, and the message is heard through the word about Christ."

Sex Is Pleasing: Temporarily When Done Wrong and Eternally When Done Right

Sex is palatable and pleasing but not necessarily right all the time. It appeals to almost every creature, and it has also brought down many mighty and noble people. One of the greatest destructive forces of Satan is sex. While sex has been used by the kingdom of darkness for theft, destruction, bondage, and death, the Kingdom of Heaven is also using sex for unity, healing, awareness, multiplication, and character building. God created sex in such a way that it gives pleasure, which is the main reason why people are finding it difficult to hold when it comes to sex. It is pleasurable and desirable, God made it so. And when undertaken in a legitimate holy atmosphere, it is a wonder of pleasure and fun. God is pleased with sex, and it gives Him pleasure to see the unity of His creation.

Perversion temporarily feels good. Perversion feels good at the moment, but the end result is always hell and tears. When sex is misdirected, no matter how much good it feels, experience has shown that the end is always trouble. Proverbs 16:25 says, "There is a way *that seems* right to a man, But its end *is* the way of death." The way of perversion seems and feels good in the interim but the end thereof is the way of death, destruction, regrets, and confusion.

Every form and act of perversion has a demon, a foul unclean spirit behind it. All sexual perversion has demons marketing and pitching the acts to others. Do not allow the evil spirit to satisfy his evil desires thru you!

A virgin spirit can be restored

The beautiful thing about God is that He is the God of restoration, the God of forgiveness and the God of a second chance. No matter how bad our lives have become, no matter how deep we have gotten sunk in the slough of sin, if we repent and genuinely seek His forgiveness, He will hear us from heaven, forgive us, cleanse us, give us a second chance, restores us and refurbishes us.

A virgin spirit can be restored through the love of God. 2 Corinthians 5:17 says, "For if any person be in Christ, He is a new creation, old things have passed away behold all things have become new."

Deliverance can restore a virgin spirit for intimacy. Sometimes, God will offer instantaneous healing, and sometimes the unity of marriage will bring forth the deliverance.

You may not know that you have a problem. You may not stay up crying at night because of horrific flashbacks or dreams. You may be married and living a somewhat satisfied life of intimacy with your spouse, but some works of the devil are subliminal.

The Author's Story Of Deliverance From Horrors Of The Past

When I first got married, I had no idea that I had been damaged by sexual sin. I had been in relationships without understanding the consequences of sexual sin on my spirit. When my husband would attempt to show affection to me without my undivided attention, I would attack rather than receive his love. In my sleep, I would swing rather than receive affection. While I am pre-occupied (such as the case with cooking), I would be annoyed by any dual interest that my husband may have. For example, he would attempt to caress me or kiss my neck as I am cooking, and rather than accepting his affection, I would complain. When I would think about my response, I actually did not want to respond that way. I was hyposensitive (an avoider) of affection. My memories and flashbacks caused me to avoid intimacy. I enjoyed my husband's affection, but because of the inner wounds and the doors that I had opened for the kingdom of darkness, my body was being controlled by the subliminal thoughts and reactions from the past, and the fruits of the flesh were prevailing. As my husband and I began to talk about why I was responding that way, we started to communicate more about the past, we implemented understanding, and healing poured. Today, I am much more accepting of my husband's affection, and my marriage thrives as a result.

Prayer and spiritual warfare restores a virgin spirit of intimacy

Through intense prayers and targeted spiritual warfare, the vigil spirit can be restored. There is nothing that the devil has done, that cannot be undone. The purpose Jesus came was to undo all that the devil has done. If we cooperate with Him in prayer and in warfare when necessary, we can be sure that we will have the displaced part of our lives restored whole.

Persist in Spiritual Warfare

Repetition is required. In order to garner strength, stability and complete wholeness, repetition of the restoration process is required. Everyone has to place safeguards to avoid temptation and realignment with the kingdom of darkness.

Sometimes, you may have to pray more than once for deliverance. There was a person that Jesus prayed for in His earthly ministry that required Jesus to do a second prayer for him before perfect healing and restoration came. Mark 8:22-25 says:

They came to Bethsaida, and some people brought a blind man and begged Jesus to touch him. He took the blind man by the hand and led him outside the village. When he had spit on the man's eyes and put his hands on him, Jesus asked, "Do you see anything?"

He looked up and said, "I see people; they look like trees walking around."

Once more Jesus put his hands on the man's eyes. Then his eyes were opened, his sight was restored, and he saw everything clearly."

In some instances (like mine), there may be dents in a person's life that don't go all at once, and require pummeling for the rough edges to be straightened out. Be mindful. Repetition does not mean that something is being done incorrectly. (See Mark 8:22-25)

Flashbacks and Memories May Require Repetition

When flashbacks arise, it takes your dogged determination to fight your way through to complete victory. Satan in his schemes will want to continually bring flashbacks to your mind during this healing process, but through reinforcement, you can work your way out of those satanic suggestions. Seek intercessors. Seek men of God. Seek God, and don't be afraid to tell the kingdom of darkness, "You have no authority over my mind! Your time has ceased! The word of God says that I have not been given a spirit of fear, but of love, power, and a SOUND mind. I take back my sound mind in Jesus name, and I command the justice of Heaven to befall you now!"

Summary

- Freedom requires courage
- Spiritual warfare is continual
- Sex is pleasing: temporarily when done wrong, and eternally when done right
- A virgin spirit can be restored
- Prayer and spiritual warfare restores a virgin spirit
- Persist in spiritual warfare
- Flashbacks and memories may require repetition

CHAPTER NINE

ALIGN YOURSELF WITH THE KINGDOM OF HEAVEN

"But He who raised Him up from the dead will raise up us also, if we do His will, and walk in His commandments, and love what He loved, keeping ourselves from all unrighteousness, covetousness, love of money, evil speaking, false witness; "not rendering evil for evil, or railing for railing," or blow for blow, or cursing for cursing."
-Bishop Polycarp, First Century Christian Martyr

The Story Of Meghan

Meghan was a beautiful girl. She had the figure that was commonly sought after and she was highly talented in the arts. She had the ability to dance, sing, and paint.

Meghan sung in the church choir for years, and congregations would rave about her skill. She was offered many opportunities to grace stages with audiences of more than 1000 congregants.

Meghan really wanted to make singing her profession. Despite her privilege amongst the church, the majority of her invitations were unpaid, and she could not sustain the lifestyle that she desired.

She was soon offered many high-paying opportunities in night clubs, singing background for world-renowned singers, and even duets with leading superstars. Meghan took all of her opportunities into consideration. Despite her interest, Meghan had observed all of the secular offers that she received were representing unbiblical stances on sex: promoting premarital affairs, flattering female body image, degrading marriage, encouraging promiscuity, or increasing interest in adultery. While the offers offered her high visibility, and high pay, her largest desire was to remain sexually pure, to fulfill her purpose for her life, and please God.

She cried out to God, "Father, you know the number of hairs on my head. You are my Creator and the Manufacturer of my life and body. I have chosen to submit my body to you as a vessel that is dedicated solely to manifesting your will. The songs that I sing, the paintings that I draw, and the choreography that I dance, I want it to please You.

You know the needs that I have, Father. Your word says:

"So do not worry, saying, 'What shall we eat?' or 'What shall we drink?' or 'What shall we wear? For the pagans run after all these things, and your heavenly Father knows that you need them. But seek first his kingdom and his righteousness, and all these things will be given to you as well. Therefore do not worry about tomorrow, for tomorrow will worry about itself. Each day has enough trouble of its own."[4]

Father right now, I am seeking your Kingdom with all that I have and all that I am. I cancel the ploys of the enemy to use my talents and my God-given gifts to exalt his kingdom. I align myself with your will Father, and I speak into existence contracts to use my talents for your service. I speak life to stages and businesses that bring together worship services. I speak into existence records

4   Matthew 6:31-33

and audiences for them. I align myself with the promise of Jesus that if I seek the Kingdom first that all else will be added, and I thank you because I know that I can claim its manifestation now in Jesus name. Amen."

Within weeks of her prayer, Meghan started to notice many opportunities to sing at conferences. She started to send her portfolio to different ministries and she soon booked her schedule with paid opportunities. Within months, Meghan was able to sustain herself thru her touring singing career, and within the first year, she had also recorded and began selling her first album. Meghan prospered.

God Created You Good From Head To Toe

God created the body with several parts that operate and function to give mankind many abilities. We commonly discuss the body parts that are visible and common, but typically, our body's attributes, our talents, our sexual organs, and our bodies abilities to create from unseen realms things that are good or bad is only spoken of in small circles; typically not offering much differing thought. People that understand the power and value of the things that are created from our bodies typically converse with others that hold the same esteem for our creativity. People with holy matrimonies talk about sex with others who have made the same decisions and people with unholy matrimonies talk with people who have made the same decisions, therefore, the cycle continues unbroken; families repeat the cycle time and time again. Aside from mainstream broadcasting, we are not typically challenged about our views of sex and creativity, and because the media is broadcasting sex so commonly, the conversion of biblical views to unbiblical views is rampant!

We watch mainstream broadcasting and see people flaunting their bodies and intertwining high skill in their art form in an intriguing way, and we assume that because we are magnetized by the behavior that we will be able to gain the same type of acceptance. Allowing the body to be a drooled over trophy is advertised in a persuasive manner as the epitome of men and women alike. We do not see the long-term effects of the commonly exploited behaviors. Contrary to what is broadcasted, the greatest fulfillment comes from being aligned to the will of God for sex.

Meghan was presented many opportunities that could have quickly taken her career to substantial status in the music industry. She had access to superstars and their stages. She was talented and received favor as a result of it.

In Proverbs 18:15-16, King Solomon said, "A gift opens the way and ushers the giver into the presence of the great." God designed your body embedded with many gifts. God designed your body good! Even if you are not aware, He has planted within you several divine gifts that He desires to be used to uplift, empower, and exhort others. He wants you to use the gifts that He has given you to transmit love and draw others to Him.

Have you ever bought someone a book that they used as a cup holder? Have you ever bought clothes that they never wore? Have you ever offered to buy someone dinner and they wasted the meal? When you buy something for someone, you take a valuable possession of yours, and exchange it for something that you presume is desirable to the other person. When they misuse what you've bought or belittle the act, it does not feel good, it's disappointing, and has a close likeness to betrayal.

God has placed value within you

He made you good. Every limb of your body has a purpose. Every hair of your head is a perfect accent. He created tiny follicles, pores, creases, and crevices; all for a purpose. When you misuse your body and direct people to darkness, it is disappointing to God. He did not bestow gifts upon you for the purpose of evil.

When Meghan was presented with many offers that could transform her career, she redirected her attention on God's will for her body. God gave her the ability to sing. He gave her favor in the eyes of men and women, so people observed her, and said, "She is beautiful". It was no deed of her own that had given her the favor and the gifts that she had, but they were all placed there by God. She came upon a choice: to do God's will or to serve her immediate ambitions? She could have adorned her body in a way that would be of greater benefit to those who had offered her opportunities, but she looked higher up at God of all.

When quick fixes present themselves that require the use of your body, ask yourself, "Would my actions inspire others to eat the fruit of the Spirit or the fruit of the flesh?" Your body was designed to encourage others to eat the fruit of the Spirit (love, joy, peace, forbearance, kindness, goodness, faithfulness, gentleness and self-control). Your gifts were designed good and they will make room for you before kings (as was foretold by King Solomon), but you want to sit before kings who offer you greater experiences to do good for others and please God. Your body is good to the senses. It can be used to hypnotize and entice people towards evil, or to draw people to good.

In Exodus, the Israelites were instructed very precisely on how they should build the Tent of Meeting. This was the place where the presence of the Lord would make Himself known. There were rules about who could enter the tent and be in such close proximity to the presence of God. There were garments that should be worn, there were sacrifices, and cleansing requirements before entrance. The Bible likens the physical meeting place of God with the physical body calling our bodies a temple. Our bodies have certain parts that are held with greater honor because of their creative abilities, and their effects on our world's future. Our sexual organs have the ability to create communities, cities, and countries of the next generation's populace.

In chapter four, we saw that from Sean and Juliyah came almost one hundred people within three generations and one lifespan. In the Bible, we see many more occasions of the population growing as a result of one couple and their sexual choices.

Take high esteem to your body and the people that you share its creative parts with. Whether you are sharing intellectual property or a sexual experience, you are participating in a divine attribute that was given to you because God made you in His image. Treat your sexual organs with greater honor than precious metals because from them come the next generation; people that are worth far more than Earth's matter can convert for currency. Do not allow anything to pollute your lineage! Do not allow satan's unholy matrimonial ties to secrete wickedness into your lineage. When the union is created, the very fibers of your lineage are affected, and the evils affect many generations. For this reason, God warned us in Exodus 34:6-7 saying:

"And he passed in front of Moses, proclaiming, "The Lord, the Lord, the compassionate and gracious God, slow to anger, abounding in love and faithfulness, maintaining love to thousands, and forgiving wickedness, rebellion and sin. Yet he does not leave the guilty unpunished; he punishes the children and their children for the sin of the parents to the third and fourth generation."

The body is to be a vessel of praise to God and a symbol of God's favor for your spouse. All of its parts are to be highly honored and well kept for his or her arrival. For this reason, Paul used the analogy of the physical body to teach lessons to the church body when he said:

"On the contrary, those parts of the body that seem to be weaker are indispensable, and the parts that we think are less honorable we treat with special honor. And the parts that are unpresentable are treated with special modesty, while our presentable parts need no special treatment. But God has put the body together, giving greater honor to the parts that lacked it, so that there should be no division in the body, but that its parts should have equal concern for each other. If one part suffers, every part suffers with it; if one part is honored, every part rejoices with it."

Every part of the body is to be treated with high regard

Clean all of the body. Treat all of the body. Groom all of the body, and adorn all of the body. Show dignity and virtuous character thru your posture and the your persistence at maintaining your temporal home.

Regarding the body, I liken God to a landlord. He created your body as a potter molds clay. He made every mark, feature, detail, hair, and change in color palette (you may perceive as discoloration); all to His satisfaction. He did not request for you or anyone else to make alterations to His artwork. He gives His stamp of approval every time you breath out and in: receiving another dose of air. He shows His satisfaction with His creation at every heart palpitation. His request is that you stay in communion by seeking Him (the Living Water) for continual cleansing, adorning yourself, and covering your honorable parts. You don't have dominion over His gender assignment for you (spoken of more in Chapter 9). Your role is merely to maximize your potential in the body that you were assigned.

The body was designed good before any exterior accents were added. Whether you have found a person to affirm your beauty or not, God created you beautiful: from head to toe, He loves you just the way that you are. If the desire for marriage has been placed in your heart, you should pray to God that He makes your beauty known to the spouse that He can align for you. Beauty is a gift. It is God's favor and it works similar to magnets: some people will have the positive and some will have the negative. Everyone will not be beholders of your beauty, but the one who does feels the privilege of God's favor. You can request for God to make your body, your voice, your scent, your touch, and your smell appealing to the man or woman that He has for you. You can honor God by keeping your sexual organs (your honorable parts) and your legacy pure thru sacred sex in marriage. As Paul said in Thessalonians 4:3-5:

"It is God's will that you should be sanctified: that you should avoid sexual immorality; that each of you should learn to control your own body in a way that is holy and honorable, not in passionate lust like the pagans, who do not know God".

God sees us when we do good and bad

The all searching eye of the Lord sees us when we do good or bad. The psalmist queried: "Whither shall I go from thy spirit? or whither shall I flee from thy presence?. (Psalm 139:7 NKJV) And the Holy Spirit through the apostle Paul added: "No creature can hide from God. Everything is uncovered and exposed for him to see. You must answer to him. " (Hebrews 4:13, God's Word Translation) When you are living right and doing good, God knows.

I liken the conscience to a two-way communication device like a phone. Romans 2:13-15 says:

"For it is not those who hear the law who are righteous in God's sight, but it is those who obey the law who will be declared righteous. (Indeed, when Gentiles, who do not have the law, do by nature things required by the law, they are a law for themselves, even though they do not have the law. They show that the requirements of the law are written on their hearts, their consciences also bearing witness, and their thoughts sometimes accusing them and at other times even defending them.)"

It tells you when you are right or wrong, signaling you when you have strayed, and telling God when you have lost signal. When you are living in sin, perversion, and doing bad, that same inward monitor that tells you, "I don't think that was right", is there to report you to God. Everything is effected by the signal going off: your demeanor, your posture, your spiritual formation patterns, your relationships, and you better believe, God knows. In 1 Corinthians 8:7, Paul said:

"But not everyone possesses this knowledge. Some people are still so accustomed to idols that when they eat sacrificial food they think of it as having been sacrificed to a god, and since their conscience is weak, it is defiled."

God does not have to slay you in the spirit every day to identify whether you are doing good or bad. He has wired you; placing the conscience (an automatic device) in you that reports your status to Heaven every second of the day; however you live, act, say, and do. The Master Creator programmed you to be in communion with Him. 2 Corinthians 1:12 tells us that our consciences report to God and man. It says:

"Now this is our boast: Our conscience testifies that we have conducted ourselves in the world, and especially in our relations with you, with integrity and godly sincerity. We have done so, relying not on worldly wisdom but on God's grace."

Jesus demonstrated a portion of the potential of God's knowledge of our internal dealings in Matthew 9:4. The Bible says, "Knowing their thoughts, Jesus said, "Why do you entertain evil thoughts in your hearts?" Jesus knew their thoughts and the statuses of their hearts. God has wired you, and He knows you inside and out!

God is disappointed with our perversion

"Marriage is honorable in all, and the bed undefiled: but whoremongers and adulterers God will judge". (Hebrews 13:4) God does not put up with sin, with perversion, with anything that is evil. He always comes at it with fury. He will judge and measure to everyone according to his deeds on earth while in the body. "For we must all appear before the judgment seat of Christ; that every one may receive the things done in his body, according to that he hath done, whether it be good or bad." (2 Corinthians 5:10)

There are eternal consequences to rebellion. On several instances, the Bible speaks of the consequences of our choices to align with forces of evil. In Proverbs 17:11, it says, "An evil man seeks only rebellion: therefore a cruel messenger shall be sent against him." And, in Revelations 21:8, it says, "the fearful, and unbelieving, and the abominable, and murderers, and whoremongers, and sorcerers, and idolaters, and all liars, shall have their part in the lake which burns with fire and brimstone: which is the second death." This is God's eternal and standing order against the rebellions, against the pervert, against all who are disobedient.

Ignorance is different than rebellion

Now, it is important for us to understand that there is a difference between ignorance and rebellion, though ignorance is punishable under the law. When Jesus told the parable of the workers in the vineyard, he introduced the emphasis that it is our responsibility as humans partaking of the progressing experience of life to be wisdom and truth seekers. He said, "And that servant, which knew his lord's will, and prepared not himself, neither did according to his will, shall be beaten with many stripes. But he that knew not, and did commit things worthy of stripes, shall be beaten with few stripes. For unto whomsoever much is given, of him shall be much required: and to whom men have committed much, of him they will ask the more." (Luke 12:47-48) People are destroyed because they don't know. So we should seek to know and walk in the light of what we know.

Be willing to abide if you have found that you are not in agreement with Kingdom laws. "He who covers his sins will not prosper, But whoever confesses and forsakes them will have mercy." (Proverbs 28:13) Such is the loving forgiving grace of God. Again He says: "Let the wicked forsake his way, and the unrighteous man his thoughts: and let him return unto the LORD, and he will have mercy upon him; and to our God, for he will abundantly pardon." (Isaiah 55:7) The loving arms of the gracious forgiven God is widely opened and spread to whoever turns to Him for mercy and forgiveness through genuine repentance.

When temptation surfaces, do as Meghan did, be honest with God. Tell Him, "God, I know that you created all. Your will is …..your promise says that if I do …, then you will do...I am experiencing temptation in the areas of…, and I want to uproot the torment that I am experiencing in Jesus name. I am petitioning for opportunities to use my talents to align with your will in Jesus name."

God can make your sex better

The word of the Lord said: "Behold, I will do a new thing, Now it shall spring forth; Shall you not know it? I will even make a road in the wilderness And rivers in the desert." You may see a pattern of intimacy that is boring, uncomfortable, or even worse, painful, but God can bring you a new thing! He can make you new! He can make your spouse new! He can make your intimate experience together new! Isaiah 43:19 repeats the concept saying, "He who sat on the throne said, "Behold, I make all things new." Trust it! Hold onto His word, repeat it, do not let any words of discouragement take them away from you.

There is nothing He cannot do. The almighty Holy Spirit of God can breathe new life, vigor and vitality into your sex life. God is able to do just what He say He will do, He is going to fulfill every promise He made as long as we don't give up on Him. The breath of the almighty can restore your sexuality and make it new again with resurrection life.

Your relationship with God can break obstacles and hindrances to sex. When God comes into a place or a relationship, change is certain and guaranteed. I always tell people that a man who loves the Lord genuinely will always know how to love a woman. The moment we learn to accept and to receive the Love of God and from God, we will also know to receive and to give love from and to our spouses.

Healthy viable relationship with our spouse is conditioned on a healthy viable relationship with God. The time we spend in knowing God will pay off in our relationship. God's word gives information about sex. The word of God, the Bible is an encyclopedia; everything about anything is in it. In it is the very foundational information for sex and sexuality that we need.

Increase your Bible intake to increase your sex enjoyment

The more that you take intake of the word of God in the area of sex, the more enjoyable our sex life becomes. This is because the word of God is more than information, it is transforming power; and it has power to produce what it talks about.

Prayer, Meditation, and Affirmations can make sex better (even if it is good now). The Scripture says in Joshua 1:8 that "This Book of the Law shall not depart from your mouth, but you shall meditate in it day and night, that you may observe to do according to all that is written in it. For then you will make your way prosperous, and then you will have good success." This includes success in our sex and love life; success in all affairs and business of life.

Pray for increased attraction

Proverbs 21:1 says, "In the Lord's hand the king's heart is a stream of water that he channels toward all who please him." Your spouse's heart is in the hand of God, and your prayers can impact their attraction. Whatever you want in your relationship, you can effect thru prayers, even increased attraction. Pray for increased results. The same goes for increased results. Prayer can make you produce more results in your life and sexuality. Pray together and pray apart. Prayer should intersperse with every aspect of your sex life. Whether you pray together or pray apart, you should pray.

The book of Esther tells of the outcome of God's favor. King Xerxes had sent his wife, Queen Vashti away because she did not submit to his order to dance for him before his company. The King then sent word out to all of his reign-a world power and a very large populace of people-the kingdom of Persia, and many women responded. Despite the numbers, the talents, the personalities, the wardrobe, the economic status, the affiliations, or any other factors, Esther won favor in the eyes of the king. Esther was an orphan from the ethnic group of people who were currently in captivity in the kingdom of Persia, so it is miraculous that she received the favor of the king, and became his bride. We know that it was not connections, cosmetics, wardrobe, money, or any other factors that gained Esther this favor. It was simply God who placed the favor in King Xerxes's heart, and because of it, she used the king's love for her to grant liberty to the Jewish people. You can pray for the same favor in the eyes of your spouse as Esther had in the eyes of King Xerxes. (See Esther 2) Songs of Solomon 2:2-3 says:

"She: 'Like a lily among thorns is my darling among the young women.'

He: 'Like an apple tree among the trees of the forest is my beloved among the young men.'"

Ask God to give you the attraction that makes you one of a kind in the eyes of your spouse. As the Shunnamite woman and Solomon coordinated, she said you are rare among the men (like a lily among thorns). And, he replied, you are rare among women (like an apple tree of the forest). When extrapolated, the statements mean so much more than that. We know that apples are fruitful and in comparison to other trees, apple trees are beautiful and yield delightful nutrition. We also know that lilies are noticeably more beautiful, pleasant smelling, and enjoyable to have than thorns, so pray that God would bestow this favor on you. Say, "Father, I know that you placed favor in the eyes of King Xerxes, so that when he looked at Esther, he was more delighted by her than all of the other women. I know that you direct the hearts of kings as streams of water. I ask right now that you would take the heart of my spouse (or state your spouse's name), and ignite a one-of-a-kind attraction in it. Just as King Solomon and the Shunammite woman spoke of a peculiarity between their love and all others, I ask that you would make an outstanding difference between me and all others in the eyes of my spouse now. I ask that you would make a peculiarity amongst my spouse and all others in my eyes now. I thank you Father because I know that your will is for me to be fruitful and multiply. I know that your will is for me to prosper and not perish, and I align myself with your will now. May your Kingdom come and your will be done thru my body, my marriage, and my offspring in Jesus name. Amen"

Defy flashbacks by forgiveness

When those satanic suggestions and reminders come to you, you should remind yourself of the forgiving grace of God through His word. By quoting to yourself scriptures that affirm and remind you of God's love and forgiveness, you will be able to defy and to drown those satanic flashbacks. Don't forget that the word of God is like a hammer that breaks the rock into pieces.

- **Forgiveness of yourself**

If God has forgiven you, and you refuse to forgive yourself, then, you are stagnating your own future. I think one of the hardest things for people to do is to forgive themselves. But you have to let go of your past so that you can embrace your today and create room for the future.

- **Forgiveness of those involved in your memory**

As you continue to walk your way through this refurbishing process, you have to also learn to forgive those who caused you pain and ordeals. If, for instance, you were lured into fornication by a friend or family member, you have to let go of that person in order to establish and enjoy the fullness of the healing process.

Summary

- You are fearfully and wonderfully made
- Your body is your temporal home embedded with good gifts that should be used to please God
- God designed you the way that He wanted you from head to toe
- He makes sex enjoyable on Earth
- God sees us when we do good and bad
- God is disappointed with our perversion
- Pray for increased attraction from your spouse
- There are eternal consequences to rebellion
- Ignorance is different than rebellion
- Align with God by adhering to the Kingdom laws
- A virgin spirit can be restored

CHAPTER TEN

USE MODESTY TO INCREASE SENSATION

"Science has shown that certain parts of the body are inherently sexual. Not because of our culture, but because of the biology God gave us. Pheromones (we call them airborne hormones) can have a major effect on others: they are what cause women who live together to "cycle" together, and they cause a man to have a slight rise and fall in his sex drive that follows his wife's cycle. There are certain parts of the body that emit large amounts of these sexual pheromones: the underarms, the genitals, the aureoles of men and women, and the navel of women are the "biggies." When these parts of the body are covered with clothes, the clothes capture most of the pheromones; when we are naked, the quantity of pheromones reaching others rises significantly. Therefore, being nude means you are sending a lot stronger sexual signals to those around you."

-site.themarriagebed.com

The Story Of Shalom

Shalom was a 25-year old virgin. She had been raised to value sexual purity. Her parents were very stringent about keeping her pure. Shalom was one of fifteen children, but none of them had seen one another without clothes. Their parents were very particular about covering body parts that released high pheromones, so the only place that nakedness could be revealed was in the bathroom for showering, changing, using the bathroom, or cleaning up. Otherwise, all of the children roamed the house clothed from shoulder-to-knee. Shalom and her siblings also had to cover their upper arms to prevent the exposure of themselves and others to the hormone release of their underarms. "Everything in between the shoulder and the knee is off limits for everyone except for your spouse!" Shalom's parents would say. "We want happy couples in our lineage, so we do our best to keep our children pure".

Near her 26th birthday, Shalom began courting with a man of God named David. He had also been keeping himself pure until marriage. They vowed that they would not hold hands until they were engaged, and they would save everything else for marriage. When they held hands for the first time, they could not get enough! They would caress one another's hands; gazing at each other with excitement. They felt like holding hands was a privilege! At their wedding ceremony, they shared their first kiss before their friends and family, and their excitement was beyond words. Their entire wedding album showed their faces smashed together like bricks and mortar. They described the sensation of being touched intimately for the first time as, "Heavenly". Shalom said:

"I had never been touched between my shoulders and my knees, I had always been clothed there, so even wind did not touch me. When my husband touched me for the first time, it was like starting a fire, and he did not even have to put a lot of pressure or effort! I was ticklish, sensitive, and on cloud nine all at the same time!"

Sex for the first time was a supernatural experience for David and Shalom. As they lay naked before one another and God, they made an eternal covenant; vowing dedication of their bodies, their union, and everything that comes from them to God's service. They said, "No textbook, scripture, or other verbiage can describe the move of God that takes place when a man and woman who are pure of spirit come together as one. It is truly miraculous. It feels as if we have never been complete, but when we consummated our marriage, we became complete and whole."

Safeguard your body for your spouse

I believe that everything that God created is to be venerated, sex much more inclusive. Sex should be consecrated, set apart, held in holy awe by all people-married and unmarried alike. Anything that is dedicated is set apart for a holy use, for a particular purpose, and this is the way God intended sex to be. Every custom and people have their own way of venerating sex, and I believe it should be done much more in our contemporary time and culture.

The Scripture says that He who created them, created them male and female, and when the two come together, they attain divine capabilities. One thing that is divine about God is that He has the ability to create something from nothing. He created man from the matter that he created. He needed no partner. He needed no materials that He could not create. We do not have the ability to create something from nothing. From everything that we create, we rely on the matter that God previously created. To build a house, you need, matter (created by God), people (created by God), and communication (an ability created by God). For fruit juice, you need fruit (created by God), a person (created by

God), and the ability to squeeze enough fruit to meet the recipient's needs (the ideas, strength, and abilities will be given by God). I think you understand what I am saying. When a man and a woman come together in the act of sex, they add ability to their being that they did not have separately. They now can create offspring. The ability to produce fruit is a divine attribute assigned to married people by God.

When offspring are produced outside of the marriage institution, it is not how God ordained for it to be. I support this concept even more passionately because I experienced the struggle of being a single parent. When sex takes place, but the relationship is not a marital relationship (regardless of whether there is conflict or drama), it affects all parties involved. In my circumstance, we did have conflicts early on in the childrearing process. We did not agree about which car seat to get (the cheaper one or the crash-tested safer one), which events were more important to attend (the child's birth or a family barbeque), and the list goes on. As a result of the differences in values, we decided that being in a marriage relationship would not work. My son was not aware of any disagreements that we had. We were always a large geographical distance apart. After the first four years of my son's life, we did not have much drama or arguments (even in isolation). Despite the appearance that everything is going peacefully, there is still consequences that we each face.

For me, I experience the emotional roller coaster of sending my son across the country annually to spend time with his dad. I have to explain to my son why the relationship did not work in a way that still keeps him open to marriage and purity in the future. I have re-married, so I have to affirm my husband, and let him know that despite the fact that I did not stay pure before marriage, he is the best. I had to overcome inner turmoil as the relationship did not work, and as I found myself in the place of a single mother, a place that I NEVER wanted to be. I would tell you more consequences, but I cannot think of them all, and I am unsure if I have identified all of the subliminal consequences. However, I can tell you that I deal with the consequences of the decision to have sex outside of marriage daily, and I highly advocate that you do it God's way.

Modesty increases sensation: for single and married people alike

Modesty in everything increases pleasure and longevity, hence God's specific instruction for us to be moderate in all things and at all time. When you cover areas of your body, when they are touched, the sensation is heightened. The part of the body that we give proper care and attention always feels good and better when indulged. For instance, a person that keeps his or her virginity will find the greatest joy and pleasure when the time for their body to be explored by their lawfully wedded spouse.

Proverbs 4:23 says, "Carefully guard your thoughts because they are the source of true life" (CEV).When your mind is guarded from ill dressed or ill spoken people, it increases your value and enjoyment of your spouse. Whatever you give value to; you cherish and set apart. God always loves you. However, when you value what God values, He cherishes you and sets you apart. He adds to you favor in the things that you have aligned to His will. Many conflicts that await people who did not wait (such as myself) will not await you if you exercise your self-control muscle. You will enjoy your spouse physically, spiritually, emotionally, intellectually, and socially. You will not compare how they do things, how they say things, how they touch you, how they make you feel, or how they look with people that have breached the sacred territories. You will be able to achieve unsurpassed satisfaction that people who have not waited will have to war to achieve. Guard the gates to your soul!

David and Shalom cannot tell you the difference between one another and other men or women in a sexual context because they never had anyone else. That increased their pleasure for sex when the right time came, and they became indulged legally.

Alleviate Negative Comparisons with Modesty

If you guard your senses (your eyes, your ears, your smell, your touch, and your taste) from intimate interaction with the opposite sex, you will not know what other men or women look like unclothed or in intimate affairs. Therefore, the treasures of your spouse become even more valuable. You are not saying, "I saw a six-pack of abs on this magazine. Why doesn't my husband have that?", or, "I saw perky boobs on TV. Why doesn't my wife have those?". You won't have any basis for comparison, and you can get satisfaction from the spouse that God has gifted to you.

You will not have a standard from outside of the home. The standard you have is the standard you have created for yourself and by yourself. You may have influences, but you create the standard. What you know is a product of teaching. You will be able to enjoy your spouse when you guard your mind.

You will not speak to your spouse with venomous speech. Because of what you know about yourself, what you learn about your spouse, and the sacredness of your bond, you will be careful about the things that you say. You appreciate each other and do not speak fowl about your patterns and behavior. You celebrate each other instead of talking down and fowl on each other.

Set clear boundaries

The beginning of the Bible tells us God's system when He created the world. It says that it was without form, then He created light with the spoken word. The second thing that He did was to separate light from darkness. With the system of God in mind, we know that when we create or when we obtain something good, we must make boundaries so that the good thing can be well maintained. Your senses are portals to your soul, and you must maintain the purity of your soul, therefore, you have to guard your portals.

• Control what you hear

Many people lose the ability to control their thoughts and achieve success because they have welcomed a compromising view thru the auditory gates of their soul. The ears are a portal that can welcome good or bad company: angels or demons. Job 34:3 says, "For the ear trieth words, As the mouth tasteth meat". What we hear is as strong and powerful as what we eat. It can be nutrition or poison for the soul. Music and conversation can alter your view of what life should be. Music is a compiled art form with a spirit behind it. Some music has words clothed in melody, and conversations are words wrapped in the spirit of the conversationalist. Other music, is clothed in tempo and pitch that can sway your emotions by the intonation of the musician. Music can be highly influential because it can be internalized by the autonomic brain system. It does not require focus. Music can effect you while you sleep. Therefore, you must be careful with the music that you entertain because you want to maintain control of your thoughts, and music can seductively relinquish control of your mind.

You may be as I was; going thru a phase where you say, "What you listen to does not have that much impact?". I understand. I was there. I listened to whatever had a nice beat, so that I could dance. I tried to be open and accepting of others, so I did not redirect conversations as much as I could. After awhile, I noticed that words that were not habitual for me to use became infiltrated in my mind. I was questioning myself, my capabilities, and my self-image was somewhat deconstructed. Thoughts that I did not allow to tempt me prior became a probable idea as time went on, and with much repetition, my lifestyle had changed focus; from eternal/legacy-building things to temporal and obligatory things.

In the digestive process, the food is taken in the mouth, chewed and mixed with saliva, transferred to the intestines, squeezed for healthy nutrients, waste is discarded, and the good travels thru the body for energy. Each part of the digestive system must work for this process to take place well. Exercise must be added, a balance of food groups, and caloric intake considered; all of these factors ensure maximum health of the body. When food that does not have nutritional value is taken in, you may not notice right away the effects that it has on your body, but with repetition, your body will change; possibly showing signs of fatigue, then progressing to weight gain, and increasing in severity.

Similarly, your auditory diet must be taken into consideration. When content goes in that is in line with the word of God, it is transported thru the mind, taken to the soul, and brings vitality to the body. Each part of the auditory digestive system must work for this process to take place well. Bible intake must be added, a balance of social, intellectual, spiritual, emotional, and physical exercise must be added to maximize the benefit of your auditory diet. When intake goes in that opposes the word of God, you may not see the signs of change to begin, but with repetition, you begin to manifest uncertainty about life, discouragement from fulfilling your purpose, a change in self image, relationship disorders, and the symptoms increase in severity.

Words are spirits. Talk can ignite unholy passion, so you must keep your gate guarded well, and maintain a good auditory diet. Jesus said: "the words I speak to you are spirit and they are life". The Bible says, It is better to hear the rebuke of the wise, than for a man to hear the song of fools. (Ecclesiastes 7:5) As painless and innocent as we try to talk ourselves down and believe that words, music, and things that we hear may be, the truth is there is TREMENDOUS power in the things that we hear. Here is a 3 step process for digesting what you hear (which should also be applied to all other portals to your soul):

1.   Choose your environments with wisdom

Although, you have permission to go everywhere, you have to decide which places are best. Some environments will not be productive or encouraging to your life purpose. Others, will be a fertile ground for healthy connection, conversation, and great auditory nutrition.

I love to dance. At one phase of life, my interest in dancing led me to club-like environments. Dorm parties, house parties, and so on. In that environment, the language was focused mostly on superficial things like, "Look at how that girl looks", or "look at how that boy looks". At times, the conversations were even more perverse or even violent. None of the conversations or music was good nutrition to my soul, however, it does add relatability to my life story.

In another phase of life, when I had joined the military, and entered basic training, I saw the auditory diet changed from destructive to constructive. In the first weeks, you are told that everything you knew may be wrong, that your initial responses to things may be wrong, you are screamed and yelled at. All of the screaming and yelling can makes you think that screaming and yelling is okay. Subliminally, you are taught about the treatment of people: speaking less than one inch from the face of the other person at high volumes is okay with authority. The subliminal thoughts that I learned at that time compromised my true ethics and thoughts of how people should be treated.

2. Decide what intake do you need to make your next step towards advancement in live

You know your assignment in life, and if you don't, check out this post or this book. With your life assignment in mind, you must decide, "What book should I read to help me get to my next step? What audio can I listen to that can help me overcome my present obstacle? Where can I get the next idea that I need to step into my next stage in life? Then, you focus your auditory diet around building and preparing yourself for your future.

For me, I listen to audiobooks in my car, sometimes uplifting praise or worship music. At home, as I am cooking, I may turn on a video or podcast that will give me good nuggets that I can use to construct a better future. While I am writing (such as the case with this blog post), I sit in complete silence, so that I can focus, and make sure that I am delivering my best. At times, I may get distracted by something. Like when I go to Youtube, and it shows, "Popular new videos", if one is enticing enough, then I will be tempted to click on it, but when I remind myself, "Tiffany, you are supposed to be focusing on your future", then I can change the momentum from being deterred into unproductivity.

3. Make auditory goals and disciplines that will advance you to success

What is the block that is stopping you from making forward movement towards your destiny? Is it connections? Is it wisdom? Is it money? Where can you gain what you do not have? Maybe a networking event? Maybe a book? Maybe an online course? Maybe a retreat or live event? Maybe a church or church service? Make goals and disciplines. Say, "I will listen to _____ amount of audio that will help me to _____ by _____", and stick to it. Be consistent about your auditory intake; ensuring that what you are putting in is helping your to advance. Add more intake as needed because you will go thru seasons where more or less is needed. Be watchful, and give your soul what it needs.

Job 34:3 says, "For the ear trieth words, As the mouth tasteth meat". What we hear is as strong and powerful as what we eat. It can be nutrition or poison for the soul.

In the digestive process, the food is taken in the mouth, chewed and mixed with saliva, transferred to the intestines, squeezed for healthy nutrients, waste is discarded, and the good travels thru the body for energy. Each part of the digestive system must work for this process to take place well. Exercise must be added, a balance of food groups, and caloric intake considered; all of these factors ensure maximum health of the body. When food that does not have nutritional value is taken in, you may not notice right away the effects that it has on your body, but with repetition, your body will change; possibly showing signs of fatigue, then progressing to weight gain, and increasing in severity.

Similarly, your auditory diet must be taken into consideration. When content goes in that is in line with the word of God, it is transported thru the mind, taken to the soul, and brings vitality to the body. Each part of the auditory digestive system must work for this process to take place well. Bible intake must be added, a balance of social, intellectual, spiritual, emotional, and physical exercise must be added to maximize the benefit of your auditory diet. When intake goes in that opposes the word of God, you may not see the signs of change to begin, but with repetition, you begin to manifest uncertainty about life, discouragement from fulfilling your purpose, a change in self image, relationship disorders, and the symptoms increase in severity.

Words are spirits. Talk can ignite unholy passion, so you must keep your gate guarded well, and maintain a good auditory diet. Jesus said: "the words I speak to you are spirit and they are life". The Bible says, It is better to hear the rebuke of the wise, than for a man to hear the song of fools. (Ecclesiastes 7:5)

Music and conversation can alter your view of what sex should be. Music is a compiled art form with a spirit behind it. Some music has words clothed in melody, and conversations are words wrapped in the spirit of the conversationalist. Other music, is clothed in tempo and pitch that can sway your emotions by the intonation of the musician. Music can be highly influential because it can be internalized by the autonomic brain system. It does not require focus. Music can effect you while you sleep. Therefore, you must be careful with the music that you entertain because you want to maintain control of your thoughts, and music can seductively relinquish control of your mind.

- Control what you see

Similar to the influence of the things that you hear, the things that you see can also change your perspectives on sex. The power of sight is one of the greatest powers in the world. Your mind can be influenced intentionally and unintentionally thru your sight, so put a guide on what you watch. For many, beauty, worth, and achievement is determined by something that can be seen. Perceptions can be inflated or deflated by the power of sight.

I remember going on vacation to see a friend of mine. I stayed in her home and everything looked well kept. When others came over, they made comments to her like, "When did you get all of this furniture?", Over the duration of my trip, I learned that she rented a house full of furniture to inflate my perception of her thru the power of sight. By her having a house full of furniture, she thought that it would add to my thoughts of her character, value, or the significance in the relationship. Rather than inflate my view of her, I perceived her as attempting to tell me a lie or live one. I saw an expression of inadequacy and discontentment. Why would she be happy with what she had? Why would she go out of her way to make this impression for me?

Looking at others can unintentionally change your thoughts towards yourself: positive and negative. It's the thoughts connected with the visual picture that can change your perception. Galatians 6:4-5 says:

"But let every man prove his own work, and then shall he have rejoicing in himself alone, and not in another. For every man shall bear his own burden." (Galatians 6:4-5)

Similar to the auditory digestive process, the eye is also a portal to your soul, and you must guard and digest everything that goes thru it. Like the security guard at the entrance to a military base, you must examine everything that goes thru your portals, so that you can focus your thoughts on advancement, progress, and manifesting your divine assignment. What you watch and who you watch will affect your thought patterns, and it will show in your thought and behavior patterns.

People all over the world have their idols; people they watch and want to be like. And if peradventure a person's idol has unholy behavior patterns, and the person chooses to follow their actions, then the person will transform their behaviors too.

Pictures and images can uplift or corrupt. For this reason, many ascribe to the power of visualization: placing images of their destined future in places that they commonly see. Much proof has been broadcasted about how the power of visualization and life-mapping can help you to achieve your goals. Healthy images produce healthy living; and dirty images produces dirty lives and unhealthy living.

Images such as those of porn damage the mind and body. Porn reprograms the mind with "what should be." Sexually explicit images can do subliminal damage when the portals to your soul are left unguarded.

- Control your thoughts

Your thoughts provoke your actions. Your actions compiled create your future. Do you want success or failure? The Scripture is definite about what you should think about:

"Whatever things are true, whatever things are noble, whatever things are just, whatever things are pure, whatever things are lovely, whatever things are of good report, if there is any virtue and if there is anything praiseworthy -- meditate on these things". (Philippians 4:8)

Noble thoughts lead to noble actions. Noble actions compiled leads to a noble future. You are not supposed to let your thoughts wander about or linger on everything. You have the power of mind management.

You are fearfully and wonderfully made. God expects you to think and reflect on how you can contribute, advance, and uplift His creative masterpieces. You and I are two amongst the estimated 7 billion people on the Earth that can be transformed thru good or bad intention.

God designed partnership and it is not contingent on you altering your body. We hear of the Seven Wonders of the World, and we have never given much thought to the greatest wonder of the wonders of the world-you and I. God has said: "I will dwell in them And walk among them. I will be their God, And they shall be My people." (2 Corinthians 6:16). God's walks in holy separated bodies for His glory and praise. We enjoy the best of partnership with Him when our bodies are kept and reserved for His holy purpose.

Summary

- Safeguard your body
- Modesty increases sensation

- Modesty alleviates negative comparisons
- Set clear boundaries
- Control what you hear
- Control what you see
- Control your thoughts

CHAPTER ELEVEN

DO NOT ACCEPT EVERYONE'S INPUT ON SEX

"The righteous choose their friends carefully, but the way of the
wicked leads them astray."
-Proverbs 12:26

Armando was born and raised in a middle class family in
Brazil. He was a handsome man and girls had always been
flocking to him. He would tell them, "I am waiting for
my wife!". At age 18, he left for the military, and met a beautiful
young woman named Viviana. He and Viviana had joined the
military on the same day, and they were both set to depart for
more training within two months of meeting. Knowing that he
and Viviana were soon to separate, Armando began to think about
how to keep his relationship with her forever.

Armando started to seek advice from his male friends. He said,
"I really love Viviana, but I have never been with a woman before.
I want her to know how special she is to me." His friends would
say, "You can't marry her without knowing anything about sex!
Brother, people from the area where Viviana is from are experts in
sex. If you want her, you need to know what you are doing. Most
of the men over there take medications to make themselves larger.
How will you stand up against what she is familiar with?"

Armando decided to begin watching pornography, so that he
could learn some things to please Viviana. Every night, he would

watch pornography and take notes, so that he could be better for Viviana. He purchased medication for enlargement and noticed a measurable difference between his erections before and after the medication. He was sure that Viviana would be happy with his newfound discoveries.

Before Viviana left, Armando gave her a promise ring. He said, "I promise that I will come wherever you are and make you my bride. I love you and I want to spend the rest of my life with you." Viviana agreed and left for her next training station.

After six months, Armando visited Viviana. They decided to marry while he was there. When they had sex for the first time, he kept saying, "I watched this video that said this should feel good to you". She would say, "Why can't you just explore my body without comparing something that you have learned on a movie?" Armando could not clear his mind from what he saw, so Viviana was upset and unsatisfied with their first sexual encounters in marriage. Before sex, he would take the medication, and he would get really aggressive; desiring continuous sex for more than 4 hours! Viviana had never had sex before, so the enlarged penis was painful for her, she wanted to explore one another's bodies, but Armando was very aggressive for penetration as he had seen in the porn videos. Viviana began to avoid having sex with Armando, and the two of them became very frustrated about the topic. Armando went to his pastor and asked for prayer. He said that the pornopgraphic images were continuous in his mind, and he keeps trying to change the faces, and try the positions and actions on his wife, but she has gotten upset and unsatisfied. They prayed and his mind was clear. He stopped taking the medication. Armando and Viviana began experimenting to find one another's likes and dislikes. They began enjoying sex.

Be Careful Of The Input You Accept About Sex

Not everyone will have the same values for sex. God has given each of us freewill, therefore, you must watch the people that you keep around you. Prune relationships that encourage non-biblical views of sex. The relationship will no longer be healthy and beneficial to your goals.

Be watchful when you enter into opposite-sex relationships with probable motives. Relationships were designed to uplift, empower, and increase, but when the fruits of the flesh (sexual immorality, impurity and debauchery; idolatry and witchcraft; hatred, discord, jealousy, fits of rage, selfish ambition, dissensions, factions and envy; drunkenness, orgies, and the like) are reasons for entering into sexual relationships, it always yields bad fruit. When the lust for sex is the reason for entrance into a relationship, the relationship becomes a product of selfish ambition: concerned about what can make you feel better and how much more can you get from the person. Lust approaches situations as a taker rather than a giver. Pride makes you enter into relationships for how it would make you look or how you can surpass everyone else. Hatred makes you enter into relationships for revenge. Those whose relationships are inspired by hatred say things like, "If he/she had not done…, then I would not be doing this to them." Sometimes, haters hold grudges towards populaces of people (for example: races, ethnic groups, genders, etc.), but demonstrate their hatred by entering into a relationship with the intent to disgrace the individual for their cause. Be careful of entering into relationships inspired by the fruits of the flesh because bad trees cannot grow good fruit.

When a relationship is entered on the basis of true love, it looks gs for you and no oneit can increase its of-tionships. It is concerned about

Now you may be saying, "Conflict is not sickness", and you are right, however, the same stimuli initiates them both: the torment from the kingdom of darkness. In the same way that a gathering of faithful believers can heal the sick, a gathering of faithful believers can help you to pray for conflict solutions. Even more specific to conflict resolution, Jesus says:

"If your brother sins against you, go and tell him his fault, between you and him alone. If he listens to you, you have gained your brother. But if he does not listen, take one or two others along with you, that every charge may be established by the evidence of two or three witnesses. If he refuses to listen to them, tell it to the church. And if he refuses to listen even to the church, let him be to you as a Gentile and a tax collector."

CHAPTER TWELVE

ALLOW SEX TO BE A TOOL TO HEAL

Sex Unites, Creates, And Seals

Tanya was 18 years old when she moved out of her parent's home. She thought, "I am grown, so I can go and make decisions for myself". Her family was a devout Christian family, but she grew hypocritical of the faith because of what she perceived as hypocrisy and double standards.

In her teenage years, Tanya's pastor began raising funds for what he called "world missions". Tanya was one of the zealous youth leaders, and she was passionate about world outreach and missions, so she invested a lot of time in leading fundraising for the missions. She hosted carwashes, concerts, and other events that raised a lot of money. Collectively, the church raised over $3 million dollars.

On the day that the pastor was leaving, Tanya and many other members of the church gathered at the airport for prayer, and to see him off. Then after two weeks, Tanya saw on the news, "Pastor of Arizona megachurch uses $3million dollars of church funds to buy an opportunity to sleep with West African Queen". The church went into an uproar as they found that the pastor had fled to West Africa with hard-earned fundraising dollars to attempt an affair. Tanya and many others reformed their views of the church at large, and vowed to never invest so much effort into evangelistic efforts.

Three years later, at age 18, Tanya was leaving Arizona to experiment with what life could offer. She was a beautiful girl and began frequenting night clubs. She entertained men thinking that they were like-minded; seeking marital relationships. Two relationships later, she was pregnant, and questioning herself about life. "Where is my life going?" she would ask herself.

She decided to be intentional in hers and her daughter's spiritual growth. She disciplined herself to read her Bible, pray, and connect to a church where she could find people who would hold them accountable to growth and virtuous character. Within one year, she also met her spouse.

As newlyweds, they enjoyed one another, but her husband was disturbed by some of her behaviors. At times, when he would touch her, she would frown her face without reason. When they laid in the bed, she would rumble and fight, and her husband could not understand. Over time, she opened up about her past. Her memories caused her to be resistant to her husband's affection, but over time (with prayer and communication), they were able to heal her internal pain, and she was free to love and receive the intimacy of her husband.

Nothing unites two individuals more than sex

Nothing sustains the world populace like sex. In sex, two spirits connect, two lives flow into each other, hearts become conscious of another rhythmic beat, souls intermingle and intertwine together, bodies blend; body to body, soul to soul, blood to blood and heart to heart; intercourse you know! Sex is a blending of two lives into each other.

The closeness, level of intimacy, and companionship that is sealed and ignited in sex is transformational. When sex is willfully entered outside of marriage, it becomes very difficult to replace the breached boundary. As Ryan explained, many people keep hypersensitive memories, and have a difficult time finding the satisfaction that they perceived that they had before. When they find a slither of possibility, they continue seeking and it leads to many relationships that are entered on an unstable basis.

• Sex seals

The Bible says, "The two shall become one flesh, says the Lord God almighty. For as he who is joined to the Lord is one spirit with Him so also is one who is joined to a husband or wife is one flesh and body with him or her. " The physical sensation and display of sex is only a partial truth of what actually takes place. During sex, two spirits are also joined together by God.

In some cultures, where virginity is most celebrated, the very first night of consummation of a marriage, the man is expected to come out of that room with a white handkerchief stained with blood, proof that the bride is what she is supposed to be, she has kept herself to her betrothed, a virgin indeed, a pride to her parents and to her community clan at large. A seal is that which confirms, ratifies or makes stable and secure. It is that which guarantees or assures. The Bible shows kings sealing an agreement with a signet ring: a symbol worn on the finger, pressed into wax or a media that would change form for a substantial period of time, and a distinguished sign of agreement made by the king. It also shows how children of God made agreements and sealed agreements both in the Old and New Testaments. In the Old Testaments, covenants between mankind and God were made and sealed with blood. In the New Testament, agreements between mankind and God are made and sealed with the redemptive blood of Jesus with the exception of the marriage covenant or those agreements that are being created adverse of the Bible's instruction (more spoken on this in Chapter 3).

• Sex creates

God has designed that His world be filled with people right from the Garden of creation; and He so desire and designed that that becomes a reality through sex which causes in procreation. God made only one man and one woman and gave them the privilege responsibility to create the human family with Him. An awesome privilege! "...God created man in His *own* image; in the image of God He created him; male and female He created them. Then God blessed them, and God said to them, "Be fruitful and multiply; fill the earth and subdue it; have dominion over the fish of the sea, over the birds of the air, and over every living thing that moves on the earth." (Genesis 1:27-28).

Sex transforms the imagination

Very important parts of the future are created as two individuals lay down, allow their thoughts to roam, and invite someone into their most intimate spaces. You begin to imagine forever with someone: two destinies become one. In true marriage, the merger of two destinies is permanent: two imaginations become one until death. What you do today, tomorrow, next year, and ten years from now affects your spouse. They become a permanent part of your imagination. You have to incorporate their likes, dislikes, goals, boundaries, and other things to make your marriage a success.

Aside from imagining forever with someone, sex changes your thoughts of others. When the sexual relationship goes well, you imagine that people are good. When the sexual relationship goes bad, you imagine that people are bad. Sex transforms your view of others in relationships. You either determine the necessity for guarded behavior or loose behavior.

Sex outside of marriage is the most tragic attack against the imagination and the future. In sex outside of marriage, you begin to embrace the person's future in your plans. You carry the imagination of the other person as a part of yours. You get to know the spirit of the other person, then you desire closeness with the compatible spirit (though you may be discerning a demon spirit that also oppresses or possesses you). Sex is the product of that desired spiritual closeness. Two physical beings cannot become closer than the presentation in sex.

The most intimate attack against your imagination is sex outside of marriage because sex merges the imaginations of two individuals. Two futures, two dreams, two collections of goals, and two bodies become one. Typically, we only discuss the physical phenomenon; the two bodies merging, but sex is far more permanent than that. Because the imagination creates and sex causes this to happen, it affects far more than ourselves. Sex outside of marriage creates fruit such as lower self-esteem, lower self-worth, family/generational curses, single parenthood, divorce, emotional baggage, and these things compounded with others can yield tragic misdirection away from the destiny. Memories are very difficult to calm or erase.

Sex causes memories that affect all seven senses, which causes the recollection of the events to maintain very strong potence and details. The memories can be shameful or pleasant; both affecting the ability for you to enjoy future relationships. Often times, the memories become more inflated; causing the person to recall more sensations than what was present at the time of sex. The recollections can make them either an avoider of sex in the future or an aggressor of sex in the future; either position is difficult to align well into a marriage. When the memories are inflated and you remember having great sex before marriage, you may have certain behaviors or sensations that you desire to feel that your spouse may have to learn. It creates sexual discontentment in future sex. When the memories are bad (even traumatic), it can be very difficult to re-associate certain touch and sex as being a good thing. Sex may be avoided simply because of a bad recollection.

Comparable to when Israel was traveling to the Promised Land, you can also be wandering for excessive amounts of time towards your destiny simply because you made the poor choice of leaving your imagination unprotected and having sex outside of marriage. You cannot bring un-appointed people into your appointed place. Israel wandered for 40 years when the journey could have taken days.

Sex Causes Some To Avoid and Some To Seek

Sex causes a hyper or hypo sensation; either you become a seeker or avoider of sex after your experience. If your memories are traumatic, guilt-ridden, shameful, or just unpleasant, you may avoid sex after your experience. Sexual memories typically affect numerous senses, they are very sensitive, and they transform your future perspective on sex. Bad memories of sex typically cause individuals to become avoiders of sex. If your memories are pleasant and exciting, they may cause you to be a seeker of sex. Your stance on sex will avoid all of your relationships with both males and females. Avoiders are typically guarded about how close they step towards members of the opposite sex, they desire to maintain distance from approaches that they perceive may be sexual in nature.

Biblical Sex Heals

As you experience the wear of the day, your beliefs and thoughts are compromised by the evil of the world. Despite your heftiest guards, some things still slip thru. You may question yourself at times saying, "Do I look good in this outfit? Am I attractive? Am I making impact in someone's life? Who really cares about what I'm doing or who I am?". Many of these questions can be answered within the intimacy of biblical sex. Sex within marriage answers those questions saying, "You look nice in that outfit to me. You stand out amongst every other woman/man on this Earth. Your attractive to me, and I am more attracted to you than anyone in the world. You're making impact in my life, and I really care about what you're doing." The act of sex heals the scars that may be bleeding of self-actualization or uncertainty because as you lay in the arms of your beloved (the one who has committed to be with you until death) and you invite the God of love, your voids are filled, and you transform from being fragmented to being complete.

Summary

- Sex unites, creates, and seals
- Nothing unites two individuals more than sex
- Sex transforms the imagination
- Sex causes some to avoid and some to seek

MAINTAIN A HIGH LEVEL OF CHARM

"Sex is mostly between your ears, not your legs. The largest, most important and most active sexual organ of the body isn't a penis or vagina. It's the brain and its structures."
-Heather Corinna

Derick and Merissa have been married for almost one year. When they first met, Merissa was 5'6", 135 lbs, with a 29" waist. She would keep her hair groomed and her custom was to do her own manicure and pedicure weekly. She would perform beauty treatments on her body to increase the elasticity and smoothness of her skin, so her skin was always very soft and she always maintained a very aromatic floral scents. Merissa would exercise once per week by going to local fitness classes, and her body stayed very toned. As Carl Carlton would say, "She was a bad mama jama!"

When they first met, Derick was very particular about his body. He counted his caloric intake and he would exercise daily with added emphasis three times weekly. He was very muscular at approximately 6', 215lbs with a 36" waist. He kept his hair and beard lined up perfectly, he wore crisp, cool scents. He always dressed very sophisticated in business attire with watch, handkerchief, pen, business socks, and cufflink accents. His business was a recreational outlet for him that was doing very well, so he was very excited about his professional achievements. He walked with dignity, his head held high, his stride full of confidence, strength, and life.

When Derick and Merissa first laid eyes on one another, they were highly attracted. Merissa had not been in a relationship before, but when she met Derick, she felt in her gut, "he is the one". He would always affirm his love for how well she groomed herself: her figure, her smell, and the silkiness of her skin and hair. He was very enthralled by her diverse intellect; she could speak with intelligence about many topics and he was intrigued by her astute perspectives. Merissa was head-over-heels over Derick. She would say, "He is so handsome and he always makes me feel special. Even when his schedule is tight, he will make the initiative to let me know that I am on his mind." Within six months, they were engaged, and eight months from their first introduction, they were walking down the aisle to be married.

Within three months of marriage, Merissa was pregnant with twins, and Derick wanted her to stay home and be a full-time wife and mother. Merissa had a difficult time adjusting to the social differences in going from a highly populated social setting to daily being home alone. She began gaining weight and slowed down on her grooming patterns.

Derek stopped paying attention to his caloric intake, he started coming home late from work, and hanging out with friends more frequently. He started to gain weight, his time management skills declined, and his business income decreased. Derek stopped making sporadic calls to check on his wife, he was not depositing money in her, "Spoil yourself" account, and dropping by on his lunch breaks became history.

Merissa began to feel neglected. She would say, "Here I am pregnant and bringing two gifts into this world, and he doesn't even pay me any attention." When Derick would come home, Merissa was tired, she wore rollers in her hair with her silk cap over them, she stopped cooking dinner, and she wore baggy garments.

Derek would complain that his wife no longer dressed or carried herself in an attractive way, but Merissa complained of his inconsistent schedule. Between four and six 'o'clock in the morning, he experienced his highest sense of sexual desire. Merissa was passionate about completing her dreams and getting her "whole" rest. Derek would approach her in the mornings, touching her breasts, her inner thighs, kissing her, and attempting to insert his penis, but Merissa would get frustrated about her sleep being interrupted. She would say, "You don't want to meet my quality time needs, but you want me to wake up perky for sex? My body doesn't work that way!". Derek would fume with anger. "If you don't want to give it up, where do I get it?" he would say. Derek turned to masturbation and pornography in an effort to avoid approaching his wife. Their sex life came to a halt, they both were displeased in their marriage, and they did not know how to begin fixing it.

Know what attracts your spouse

Heather Corinna said, "Sexuality is physical and sensory, but also chemical, emotional (yes, even for anyone who says sex isn't at all emotional for them), psychological, intellectual, social, cultural and multi-sensory". Everyone loves for their senses to be elated. Sex is an atmosphere for the senses to be made to feel as they can in no other activity under the sun. Everyone has different ways of being stimulated. In his hierarchy of needs, Abraham Maslow said that everyone's basic needs are physiological, safety, love and belonging, esteem, and self-actualization. In addition to human basic needs, you have needs in order to perform at your peak sexual health. From his biblical studies and marriage counseling experience, Dr. Myles Munroe said that typically the most important male needs in marriage are sex, recreational fulfillment, physical attraction, domestic support and refuge, respect, and admiration . Contrarily, the typical order of women's needs are love and affection, companionship, honesty and openness, financial support, and family connection. Men and women have to exercise discipline to ensure that both needs are being met, your spouse is attracted, and your sexual rhythm is satisfying to the both of you. The last thing that you want is for either partner to feel raped or forced and resentment to build as a fortified wall between you. Open the lines of communication, discuss one another's needs, and compromise for mutual enjoyment.

Know The Physiology For Sex

We all have our physiological make-up. It differs from one person to another. It differs in both sexes. It is therefore your responsibility to seek to know and to understand the physiology of your spouse. A person's physiology can be sometimes unpredictable. It can be rosy and up in the morning and down in the evening; so it takes attention from both parties to decode the bodily regulation of each other. Regarding sexual appetite, it benefits you to understand your spouse's sensitive areas. Heather Corinna said:

"Typical erogenous zones include the lips, tongue, palms and fingers, the soles of the feet, the inner thighs, nipples, neck, ears, armpits and the genitals. Our skin, as a whole, is really an erogenous zone. Mucocutaneous regions of the body (made of both mucosal and cutaneous skin) are also often particularly sensitive: parts like the foreskin, penis, the external clitoris, the inner labia, the perineum, mouth or nipples. Just so it's clear, there is no absolute relationship between gender and where on your body you feel sexually sensitive: people who are or who identify as male can and do enjoy nipple stimulation, while some people who are female or female-identified do not, for instance."

Learn your sensitive areas, your appetite, know your spouse's appetite and its signs, and respond to it unreservedly. Men and women are different. It is important to keep in mind that the physiology of men is different from that of women. Typically, the woman's body takes more time to arouse sexual desire. As the saying goes, "For women, sex starts in the kitchen". She requires sporadic shows of affection preceding sex, whereas men are much quicker to become aroused.

Know what your spouse desires from sex. It is certainly most important that you discuss your sexual desires with your spouse. You should know what your spouse desires from sex. Find out what gives your spouse pleasure and satisfaction (and as long as it is consistent with scripture), give it.

Sex is not about us but about the other person. Never forget that the ultimate message that you want to transmit in sex is affirmative love. Sex is not merely about your satisfaction (that is selfishness), but it is also about the satisfaction of your spouse (that is true love, that is giving).

Hormones Change

Sex expert Heather Corinna said:

"Androgens, estrogens and progestins are "sex" hormones produced by the adrenal glands by people of all sexes, with some difference in amounts between all sexes, and also in the testes, ovaries and a couple other parts of the body. These play a part in sexual pleasure. Androgens affect the desire for sex and are one of its many drivers, though within average hormonal ranges, the brain plays a bigger part in sex drive than those hormones. Androgens play a part in erection and response of the penis, the clitoris and the vagina. For those with a vagina, estrogens influence vaginal lubrication and elasticity of vulvovaginal tissues."

Beginning in puberty, the body is beginning to transmit sexual hormones at an increased rate. The hormones change; fluctuating throughout life. Stay conscious of the effect of your intake and your circumstances on your hormones. Know that the hormone changes will affect your sexual desire.

Respect your spouse's physiology

Sex is a mind thing finding expression through the body. The body is built in a way that it can lose or gain strength. It is for you to know that you and your spouse's bodies will not always be at 100 percent output. At such times, you must respect your bodily condition and make-up.

Know the signs of fatigue or stress. Being tired can cause sex to become a frustrating topic rather than a show of love and intimacy. Sweating, blood pressure, temperature, heart rate, drowsiness, frustration, irregular posture, slow walking speed, disposition, or movement, and other signs of fatigue should signal you to show grace rather than sexual aggression. Be understanding.

Experiment for enjoyment

What seems good for you may not be good for your spouse. Sex within the confines of marriage is like a treasure hunt; always evolving and always finding new and changed sensations. The body goes thru a continual metamorphosis with age, childbirth, and changing exercise and diet habits. With you and your spouse constantly changing, you should enjoy the continual experimentation and exploration that goes along with making sex the most pleasurable experience that it can be. Sex positions, sex enhancers, attractive garments or lingerie, being attentive to times of accelerated sensation or desire, and many more things can be done to make sex playful and fun.

Sex positions can change the blood circulation, therefore alternating the sensations in the body. Similar to many other things that are not wrong, but can become wrong if the heart and intent is not aligned with love, sex positions should be an expression of love. While you may find interest in certain positions, you should not be upset if your spouse is incapable to perform that way. Some positions require a person to almost be a gymnast or to exercise in order to reach the level of flexibility and strength to maintain. You and your spouse may find interest in exercising in order to achieve more possibilities and positions, but this should be a compromise of you both. Sex positions can be fun to explore, but they need to be explored with compromise. Keep comfort into consideration. Do not put emphasis on one person needing to compromise comfort for the other to experience pleasure. Compromise. Every couple should experiment with positions as they wish, and then adopt the ones that are favorable, comfortable and pleasurable to both parties.

Elate The Senses: Start With The Sight

Bishop T.D. Jakes said, "Men are stimulated by what they see, women are stimulated by what they feel." The two senses that are typically the first to be aroused in the sexual experience are the sight and the touch. Taking care of the body is an expression of dignity. In the book of Esther, the women would go thru one whole year of body treatments before they stood before the king, and this was simply for them to be considered an optional queen. If the women would exercise this much care for King Xerxes who was only considering them an option, how much more should you exercise care to bring yourself before the king or queen of your house? The way that you take care of your body influences your spouse's sexual response to you. Ask your spouse, "What grooming habits do you like for me to maintain?" In the Songs of Solomon, we see jewelry (earrings, jewels around the neck, easily removed robes, applications made to enhance the silkiness of the skin, and massage oils) used to enhance sexual experience. You have one person in the world that you have the privilege to spend the rest of your life with. Give them the honor and excite them with your appearance and the way that you feel. Be considerate of the garments that you wear. Lingerie or body paints may be something fun to explore to add greater attraction, suspense, surprise, and excitement to your marriage bed. Ask them, "Do you like when I wear garments like this?".

Use Smell And Taste To Enhance Sexual Experience

In the book of Songs of Solomon, we can see the couple using essential oils to add scent and possibly taste. In Songs of Solomon 2:3, it says, "Like an apple tree among the trees of the forest is my beloved among the young men. I delight to sit in his shade, and his fruit is sweet to my taste." In this passage, it is not clear what parts of the body the woman was stimulating orally, but it is clear that she enjoyed the taste of her spouse's body. In this passage, we see the Shunamite woman clearly making note of her spouse as being superior to all those around. Your spouse is yours from head to toe. Make the experience pleasurable to every sense. In Songs of Solomon 4:16, the Bible says, "Awake, north wind, and come, south wind! Blow on my garden that its fragrance may spread everywhere. Let my beloved come into his garden and taste its choice fruits. Many scholars believe that the enclosed passages hint about oral sex. The passages do not clearly say what body parts were being orally stimulated, but we do understand that the couple was tasting one another's bodies. The passage also made mention of his taste being appetizing.

Some massage oils and body paints are edible, and can add a sensation as you explore your spouse for stimulating areas. Some natural ingredients such as coconut oil, essential oils, vegetable glycerin, or honey can be used to add flavor to the body while also supplementing natural lubrication. Edible enhancers and massage oils can make oral stimulation more appetizing, they can add a delight to your touch, they can enhance the scent of the body, and make sex more enjoyable for both parties. While oral sex is not directly forbidden in the Bible, some people have personal programming or convictions against it. Practices like oral sex or oral stimulation should be agreed upon by both spouses, and convictions respected.

Many people limit their exploration in sex due to scent. They may not like the smell of certain areas of the body (which fluctuate at different times of the month with hormone changes). For some, the smells that are put off by sexual hormones that can be noticed in the underarms, The Bible tells us that scent and the repetition of the name of your loved one can add delight to sex. Songs of Solomon 1:3 says, "Pleasing is the fragrance of your perfumes; your name is like perfume poured out." Find sexual enhancers and perfumes that can add attraction to your body and make sex more fun to explore.

There is a lot of preparation that are to be made in anticipation for sex. Serve your spouse, honor them, let them know that they are always important to you, keep boundaries in your time to show them that you truly care, and experiment with their sensitive areas. Satisfactory sex and love making is never impromptu but a series of preparation that climaxes into sex.

Use your talents to communicate your love

Create a love and sex environment with songs and with music. You can write poems that transmit messages of love throughout their whole body. You can express your feelings thru visual art, dance, and acting. Creativity makes sex even more fun and can add elements of expression that words cannot contain.

In his book, *The Five Love Languages*, Dr. Gary Chapman shared that everyone communicates love differently: some thru touch, some thru giving gifts, some thru words of affirmation, some thru acts of service, and others thru quality time. Discover your love language and your spouse's love language, add this to your arsenal, and make attempts to say, "I love you" before, during, and after sex in a way that they can receive.

Your marriage bed is your Holy Of Holies

"Marriage is honorable in all and the bed undefiled." I believe the most sacred place for a man and a woman in marriage is their bedroom, and the most sacred spot in that bedroom for them is the bed-the holiest of all. Dress appropriate for the Holy Of Holies. The High Priest as ordained of God cannot just come into the Holy Place casually; there is special dress and a dress pattern reserved only for the Holy Place. This is also true of marriage. There is a way partners dress to their Holy Place. Learn it if you have not. Appropriate dresses for appropriate ceremony.

Smell appropriate. The High Priest dresses and smells a particular way for the ceremony at the Holiest of all. There are particular perfumes and specially made anointing oil that the High Priest would have to wear to go into the Holiest Place. Partners, let us learn this.

Clean up before and after sex

For hygiene purposes, it is important that we clean up before and after the sex act. Use of disinfectants is important.

Infections can come from lack of internal and external cleanliness. This is why we should consciously clean ourselves with the use of bath soaps and perfumed disinfectants; in this way, we will be able to check infections.

Enter submitted to your spouse's enjoyment. The way we give ourselves unreservedly to the worship of God when we dedicate ourselves to Him, is the same way we should give ourselves to our spouse unreservedly without holding back if we are to enjoy the act. Always seek to look better, smell better, and perform better than ever before! Keep the bed exciting!

Communication increases pleasure and unity

Spouses talk to their spouses differently in their bedroom than they do anywhere else in the world. The tone, the volume, the pace, and everything else changes because of sex. Good sex is always preceded by communication and also climaxed afterwards in communication. Communication is good for viable healthy sexual relationships. It should be a desire and practice.

The Scripture has this to say about communication between partners: "The voice of my beloved! Behold, he comes Leaping upon the mountains, Skipping upon the hills…. My beloved spoke, and said to me: "Rise up, my love, my fair one, And come away. For lo, the winter is past, The rain is over and gone. The flowers appear on the earth; The time of singing has come, And the voice of the turtledove Is heard in our land. The fig tree puts forth her green figs, And the vines with the tender grapes Give a good smell. Rise up, my love, my fair one, And come away! "O my dove, in the clefts of the rock, In the secret places of the cliff, Let me see your face, Let me hear your voice; For your voice is sweet, And your face is lovely." (Song of Solomon 2:8-14)

Communicate about what you like. Communication encompasses likes and dislikes. During the process, it is important that you talk to your spouse about their likes. You may think that you know your spouse, but sex is always evolving, so you must talk about it for maximum fulfillment.

Communicate about comforts and discomforts. For instance, it is important to talk about sex positions, scents, flavors, and any other sexual enhancers that are comfortable to both parties and the ones that are not comfortable during the act. Whatever it is that makes for pleasure and displeasure should be talked about such that both parties can know the like and the dislikes of each other and then compromises should be reached that make for enjoyable sex.

Compromise for mutual enjoyment

I know of no other secret that makes for success in marriage than compromise. We all have our minds made up about how we want to indulge the sex act, but when we come to real practice we have got to know that it is not about us but about the other person; hence compromise is the only way to then merge our separate ideas into one whole pleasure that is suitable to both parties.

Communicate about "no's." Whatever is not communicated in sex is misunderstood. So it is wisdom to communicate the YES's as well as the NO's.

Summary

- Know what attracts your spouse
- Know the physiology for sex
- Hormones change

- Respect your spouse's physiology
- Experiment for enjoyment
- Elate the Senses: Start with sight
- Use smell and taste to enhance sexual experience
- Use your talents to communicate your love
- Your marriage bed is your Holy of Holies
- Clean up before and after sex
- Communication increases pleasure and unity
- Compromise for mutual enjoyment

The Divine Commission For Heavenly Sex

I trust that you have enjoyed reading thru this book and you have gained insight for how you can enjoy Heavenly sex within the confines of marriage. Purity of the soul is something that should be highly cherished inside and outside of marriage! It gives you increased sensation physically, mentally, and spiritually. Sexual purity can be restored because of the grace of Jesus Christ.

This is a biblical affirmation to repeat to restore sexual purity, reconnect in Spirit with God wholly, and increase the intimacy in sex:

Now, Lord, my God, you have made your servant a vessel of the most High God. I thank you for your handiwork, and your mindfulness of me. I relinquish all those whom I've harbored unforgiveness against now, and I ask your forgiveness for my sins. I pour the cleansing blood of Jesus Christ over me from head to toe, and I ask that my mind, spirit, soul, and flesh be cleaned.

Your word says, "Come now, and let us reason together, saith the LORD: though your sins be as scarlet, they shall be as white as snow; though they be red like crimson, they shall be as wool." (Isaiah 1:18) Restore me to full communion with You that I may also give and receive intimacy as You originally designed it. Allow me to experience the wholeness that You ordained sex to be that my marriage can fulfill the command to "be fruitful and multiply". (Genesis 1:28) I thank You for hearing my prayer. Amen.

-Tiffany Domena

ABOUT THE AUTHOR

Tiffany Domena is an Ambassador of the Kingdom of Heaven, wife, mother, bestselling author, and advocate for living your life by YHWH's design. Bringing nine years of military experience, an educational background in Bible (Bachelor's in Religion along with some graduate coursework), and a Biblical worldview, Tiffany enjoys training others on how to be successful in their deployments to the Earth. She is the founder at Kingdom of Heaven Ambassadors International where her primary focus is taking enemy territory back on the internet and in mainstream media, and refocusing hearts and minds on Yeshua the Messiah. Expertly publishing ten books, hosting a podcast, and blogging on pertinent topics that strike our world, Tiffany's passion bleeds thru her work, and encourages those who get wind of her. She has been known to speak and write on topics including prayer, life purpose, marriage, sex, temptation, goal-setting, wisdom, and prosperity. Other books by Tiffany include:

- 12 Undeniable Laws For Being Wise As A Snake
- 12 Undeniable Laws For Prayer
- 12 Undeniable Laws For Marriage
- 12 Undeniable Laws For Being A Kingdom of Heaven Ambassador
- 12 Undeniable Laws For Prosperity
- Perception: The World's Most Affluent Leader and companion workbook

- Transform Your Habits To Create Your Position of Power Workbook
- Someone Covets You

Find more resources, training, or to subscribe to Tiffany's blog, podcast, or social network, visit www.kingdomofheavenambassador.com.

ONE LAST THING...

If you enjoyed this book, I would love to hear! I personally read all reviews written on my books, and I use them to make the books better and more effective. I would greatly appreciate your feedback at the links below:

Amazon Link:

http://www.amazon.com/Tiffany-Domena/e/B00MSHE0LI

Website Link:

http://www.kingdomofheavenambassador.com/shop/

Goodreads Link:

https://www.goodreads.com/author/show/8459952.Tiffany_Domena

May God bless you!

Tiffany Domena

www.ingramcontent.com/pod-product-compliance
Lightning Source LLC
LaVergne TN
LVHW051103080426
835508LV00019B/2033